I hope you enjoy reading
this more than I did
living it!

POLITICALLY
INDICTED

POLITICALLY INDICTED

THE REAL STORY BEHIND THE JERSEY STING

ANTHONY R. SUAREZ

www.mascotbooks.com

POLITICALLY INDICTED

I have tried to recreate events, locales, and conversations from my memories of them. In order to maintain their anonymity, in some instances I have changed the names of individuals and places. I may have changed some identifying characteristics and details such as physical properties, occupations, and places of residence.

For more information, please contact:
Mascot Books
620 Herndon Parkway #320
Herndon, VA 20170
info@mascotbooks.com

CPSIA Code: PRFRE1018A
ISBN-13: 978-1-64307-143-5

Printed in Canada

This book is dedicated to my family, especially my wife, Catherine, and my mom, who stood by me every day, in my darkest hours. It is also dedicated to the residents of Ridgefield. You all are my extended family.

CONTENTS

Chapter 1: Arrested   1

Chapter 2: Entry Into Politics   9

Chapter 3: Meetings with the Devil   21

Chapter 4: Summer Vacation   33

Chapter 5: Hanging with the Rabbis   43

Chapter 6: Guilty Until Proven Innocent   53

Chapter 7: Media Circus   63

Chapter 8: Big Brother Wants to Know Where You Are   73

Chapter 9: Lawyered Up   79

Chapter 10: The Video Tape   89

Chapter 11: Fairweather Friends   99

Chapter 12: I'm Okay, You're Okay   107

Chapter 13: Keeping It Real   115

Chapter 14: Preparing the Case   121

Chapter 15: Campaign 2009 131

Chapter 16: Last Hope 141

Chapter 17: Christmas Spirit 147

Chapter 18: Indicted 155

Chapter 19: Reorganization 165

Chapter 20: The Trial 173

Chapter 21: No Appeal Necessary 181

Chapter 22: Recall Election 191

Chapter 23: Preparing for Trial 201

Chapter 24: Trial by Fire 209

Chapter 25: Vindication by Election 225

Epilogue 231

Acknowledgments 237

Chapter 1

ARRESTED

There I sat, handcuffed to a chair like the hostage of some crackpot militants. Adding to the aura of unreality, I was surrounded by a group of Orthodox rabbis, who were cuffed to their respective chairs as well. When I awoke earlier that morning at the New Jersey shore, I could not have dreamed the bizarre chain of events that brought me here. How did I, an attorney, a respectable citizen, the mayor of Ridgefield, New Jersey, end up a prisoner in this dingy room in Newark? Perhaps the rabbis were thinking the same thing. Had they asked, I would not have been able to answer. It was July 23, 2009, and the nightmare was only beginning.

I will remember the details of that day as long as I live. It began inauspiciously on Long Beach Island, where my family and I were enjoying a relaxing vacation. Away from the pressures of job and governance, I settled into a pleasant routine. I woke at 6:00 a.m. and donned shorts, shirt, and sneakers; grabbed my iPod and bike helmet; and headed out the door for a morning ride around town in solitude. The sky was overcast. It was cooler than the day before, and it looked like rain.

No matter. I had come to the shore prepared. Returning to the bedroom, I walked past my sleeping wife, Catherine, pulled a sweatshirt from the dresser drawer, and grabbed a white rain jacket. Careful not to wake my two small children, Laura and Matthew, who were sleeping soundly after a long family walk the evening before, I made my way to the front door naively believing I was ready for anything the day might now throw at me. All in all, the week was shaping up as the best vacation in our seven summers in Beach Haven.

Prepared for weather contingencies, I strolled around to the rear of the house, unlocked my mountain bike, walked across the uneven Jersey shore pebble "lawn" to the street, and pushed off, heading down to Ocean Boulevard where I followed the boulevard bike lane south, gliding by the large oceanfront houses Catherine and I often admired.

As I pedaled toward Fantasy Island, a small amusement park where on Fridays the kids got more than their money's worth with one ticket for all the rides, the temperature dropped a few more degrees and it began to drizzle. I decided to cut my usual ride short and wound my way through a maze of small streets, following the most direct route back to Long Beach Island Boulevard and then home.

I reached the boulevard at the town shopping center and rode north past a bookstore and some restaurants. Stopping for a traffic light, I rested my foot on the curb. Waiting for the light to change, I glanced at my cell phone to check the time and noticed I had three missed calls, before 7:00 a.m. Somewhat concerned, as it was unusual for anyone to call me that early, much less at three-second intervals, I immediately removed my headphones and began to listen to the messages coming from a female voice.

The woman identified herself as an FBI agent and advised that it was important for me to call her immediately. With Bruce Springsteen's "Tenth Avenue Freeze Out" faintly playing from the dangling headphones, I listened to the other messages—all from the same woman, who was desperate to speak with me immediately.

Why would an FBI agent be calling me? I wondered. The year before I had been questioned by an FBI agent and an investigator from the United States Attorney's Office regarding the Bergen County Democratic Party chairman, who was the subject of a federal probe. I thought they might be calling about another political figure who faced a possible prosecution.

Not even thinking I should confer with an attorney first, I dialed the number on my voicemail. What I heard next turned my world upside down. When the woman answered, she identified herself as an FBI agent and calmly said to me, "I'm sorry to be the bearer of bad news, but there is a warrant for your arrest."

Still convinced this must be a huge mistake, or even possibly a cruel joke, I asked, "For what?"

She refused to tell me but said I should turn on my television set to find out. She then asked me where I was. I hesitated, and she told me that she was not going to send anyone to arrest me but just wanted to know my whereabouts.

I told her I was on Long Beach Island in Beach Haven and would need to call her back. She asked me what I was going to do. "Contact my attorney," I replied.

As our conversation ended, I thought this was a terrible mistake or nasty practical joke. What FBI agent calls someone and claims to have a warrant for their arrest yet doesn't know where they are? That scenario just seemed so strange, so unlikely, but . . .

I knew I had to get home and turn on the television, so I pushed off the curb and began to pedal frantically toward the beach house.

I rode past the supermarket and turned right at Eighty-Third Street, zipped past Acme Bicycle Rentals, pulled into the small two-family house my family was renting for the week, walked the bike to the backyard, secured it, took off my helmet, and walked around to the front door in a daze. The house was crowded, since my parents had rented it as a summer surprise present and were staying with us. My wife and I had had a rough year and really needed the getaway. Catherine's father had passed away, I had to endure a baseless lawsuit from a political opponent, and our daughter contracted an illness that caused the whole family to be quarantined in a Florida hotel room. Yet we had no idea how tough things were going to get.

Everyone was still asleep upon my return, so I called my law partners, Ron Dario and Shelley Albert, to explain what was going on. They were as shocked as I was and told me that the only attorney in our office who was conversant with federal criminal law was out of the country, so I phoned the office of Henry Klingeman, a lawyer I knew who handled federal cases. My return and phone calls must have wakened Catherine. After I told her what was happening, she went into the living room to turn on the television. In between my repeated calls to Henry, the FBI agent called me again and asked what I was doing. I told her I was awaiting my attorney's call. My parents had awakened, and

Catherine filled them in on the story. They were quite dismayed. Then Catherine called me to the living room.

As I stared at the television screen, real estate developer David Essenbach, a man I had met with several months before, was identified on-screen as a "cooperating witness" in an investigation into a money laundering and kidney smuggling racket run by rabbis and political corruption involving New Jersey public officials. According to the news, the investigation had concluded with arrests that morning. I had absolutely no idea why I was being arrested for meeting with Essenbach, as I had done nothing illegal during our encounter.

While I was trying to figure out how I fit into this criminal jigsaw puzzle, Henry finally called me back. I brought him up to date on what I had learned and gave him the FBI agent's phone number. He told me he would call her and get back to me regarding our subsequent course of action. While I awaited his call, my mother and wife began to cry and my stepfather sat staring in disbelief at the television. I tried to concentrate on what the reporter was saying. A rabbi's son from Deal, New Jersey, who had been caught in criminal activity, had agreed to aid federal prosecutors in a two-year-long sting operation as part of a plea bargain. The details of the investigation were becoming clear, but I was still dumbfounded that I was being arrested for merely meeting with this disreputable man.

Henry finally called me back and informed me that the agent wanted me to surrender at the Newark FBI office as soon as possible. My stepfather volunteered to drive me up to Newark, and my wife and mother wept, which, needless to say, disturbed me considerably. I don't remember saying goodbye to my family, or even getting dressed, but I soon found myself in the car clad in shorts, Crocs, and, ironically, my "Property of Ridgefield Police Department" shirt.

On the way to Newark, my cell phone was buzzing constantly, as friends and associates sought clarification and wanted to ask how I was feeling. I could not keep track of all the calls and missed some. I tried to return at least the calls to close friends who were confused and concerned.

Although I remember speaking with many people that morning, I honestly cannot recall the details of any of those conversations. The whole trip, up the Garden State Parkway and then the New Jersey Turnpike to Newark, was like a hazy dream. The only thing that I was sure of was that I was being arrested for no apparent reason. I was still in shock, confused and concerned about my future but, more than anything else, worried about the effect it would have on my family.

On arrival in Newark, my stepfather parked the car in a lot a few blocks away from the historic old building that housed the Krovatin Klingeman firm. Henry met us as we got off the elevator, walked us to his office and began to explain what was going to happen next. Just as I was beginning to feel truly overwhelmed, two FBI agents, a male and female, appeared. I left with them, and my stepfather remained in Henry's office.

While we were walking out, I told the agents that I needed to use the restroom and abruptly learned how invasive the federal government could be. The male agent followed me into the men's room. He watched me relieve myself, and then after I washed and dried my hands, he examined the paper towel I had discarded into the waste basket.

The three of us rode down the elevator, an agent on either side of me, then walked out to the street toward an unmarked Dodge

Charger that was parked illegally. The female agent produced a set of handcuffs and told me to put my hands out. "Standard procedure," she said. Handcuffed for the first time in my life, I was hustled into the Dodge Charger as people passing by on the street stared, probably thinking they were witnessing some dangerous criminal being brought to justice.

They drove me several blocks away to a building on McCarter Highway I had often passed without realizing it was a federal building. As we approached the entrance facing the Passaic River, the female agent, in an apparent attempt to rattle me, advised me that she knew the make and model of the vehicle my wife drove. When I asked her how she knew, she said, "We're the FBI; we know everything."

This was the same woman who had frantically attempted to get in contact with me by telephone while I was on my morning bike ride. I thought to myself, "Well, wise-ass, if you know everything, how come you didn't even know where I was, or, at the very least, that I was on vacation?"

On leaving the Dodge Charger, we passed through a gauntlet of photographers taking pictures of me being escorted in handcuffs by FBI agents. These images would appear in campaign fliers printed by my political opponents over the next two years, with no regard to the effect it would have on my children.

It wasn't until I arrived at the federal prosecutor's office that I had any idea why it was so urgent that I appear in Newark that morning. Those arrested were the subjects of a carefully timed and staged media event conducted by the FBI and the United States Attorney's Office. The prosecutor's public relations machine needed a circus-like "perp walk" parade before the assembled media to kick off a press conference announcing the results of the investigation facilitated by the government's star witness, the sociopathic crook, Mr. Essenbach, who I would later learn was serial swindler and con man, Solomon Dwek. It inspired the first in a succession of stories that would dominate New Jersey's airwaves and newsprint for weeks and months on end.

On entering the federal building, we encountered a large number of people milling around and eating breakfast who stared at me as I walked in. I felt like I was on display, an investigation trophy, and now, in a metaphorical sense, the federal prosecutor's personal property. He and his staff would own me and use me for their own purposes for the next fifteen months of my life.

Chapter 2

ENTRY INTO POLITICS

atherine and I met in Hoboken during April of 1994. A friend of mine, Frank, who was working with me as a law clerk in the Superior Court of New Jersey, said he was going to meet up with a friend of his from Paramus High School who was attending Rutgers Law School. This friend of his, Lisa, was going to introduce him to a third-year law student whose first name was Catherine, and she was also bringing along some other friends from the law school. As I contemplated even going to Hoboken that evening, another law clerk, Patrick, who would become one of my closest friends, encouraged me to go to the live music club, so I agreed.

Patrick and I drove to Hoboken together, and we arrived before Frank. When I got to the club, Live Tonight, I found myself speaking with a young woman who was both funny and smart and had a great smile. When Frank arrived it was too late; I had already gotten Catherine's phone number and planned on taking her out that week. Neither of us realized at that time that we would soon be married and would raise two beautiful children, spending the rest of our lives together. We also never realized the ups and downs that would occur during the course of our marriage.

Catherine and I purchased a small Cape Cod home on Oak Street one year before we were married. It was one block away from my parent's house, where I spent most of my life. My grandfather, Anthony Suarez, who adored Catherine, helped us with the down payment, and we were just able to make the monthly mortgage with our low first-year associate salaries at the respective law firms where we were working. The house was small, cozy, and needed some work. My in-laws helped us to fix it up for almost a year before we were ready to move in.

We were married on October 20, 1996, the day after one of the biggest nor'easters we had in New Jersey up to that point in time. The day before the wedding, I sat alone in the kitchen. As I assembled the wedding programs that my college friend and groomsman Rich Lombardi created, I looked out the front window and saw rain pouring down and large tree branches swaying back and forth in the wind.

When I finished assembling the programs, I boxed them, drove back down the hill to my parent's home, and went to sleep one last time in my childhood bedroom. The next day, Sunday, I would be getting married.

The weather had cleared in the morning, and it was a beautiful fall day. We were married in the Church of the Little Flower, a few blocks from where Catherine lived with her parents in Berkeley

Heights. Catherine had grown up in Elizabeth, but the family had moved to Berkeley Heights after her grandparents both passed away. The next day we went to Hawaii for two weeks for our honeymoon and returned to Ridgefield on Election Day 1996, when Bill Clinton was reelected as president of the United States. I was happy because even though I was never really interested in politics up to that point, I believed that President Clinton was doing a great job.

I always felt bad for the way that the Republicans had treated the president, which was one of the reasons why I registered as a Democrat. Locally, the Republicans had won yet another local election, and the local governing body remained all Republican: a Republican mayor who had been there for decades and six Republican councilmembers, who did everything the mayor asked.

Catherine and I then settled into life as two married lawyers, going about our daily affairs and crazy schedules while balancing family life in between. After less than one year of being married, Catherine came to me one day and showed me an ad in the local newspaper advertising for candidates to run for Ridgefield Borough Council. It is a moment that I always tease her about, since she started to dislike politics the day I started running for public office.

When Catherine first showed me the ad, I thought it was a great idea. I was living in the town where I grew up and wanted to raise our children. Ridgefield was a town that I loved because of all that it had meant to me, and what better way to give back than to serve in public office?

The town had been run by Republicans for years. Republican Mayor Stewart Veale was viewed by his enemies as a dictator, but his supporters saw him as a savior. Mayor Veale had been a friend of my grandparents, Anthony and Rose Suarez. In fact, my grandfather had served as Mayor Veale's alternate on the library board. The Ridgefield Republican Organization was a force to be reckoned with. They had not lost an election in almost ten years, and the entire Mayor and Council was Republican.

Ridgefield's form of government is known as the borough, and it is the most popular local government among the 566 municipalities in the state of New Jersey. In short, there is one mayor and six councilpersons. The mayor serves a four-year term and the councilpersons serve three-year terms. As a result, two councilpersons are up for election every year, and the mayor's seat is up once every four years. The borough form of government is also known as the weak mayor and strong council, since the real power rests in the majority of the council in terms of taking governmental action, including hiring, firing, appointments, and lawmaking. If the mayor is at odds with the majority of the council, he or she will be relegated to performing weddings and breaking council ties.

In order to run for office, I needed the support of the Ridgefield Democratic County Committee, made up of five men and five women who represented the five voting districts in town. I also needed the support of the municipal chairman, an old time Democratic figure by the name of Jerry Plancher.

When I attended the meeting that was called for the selection of candidates by the county committee, I showed up with Catherine, and it took place in the office of county committee member and local attorney Stephen Pellino. The group was an interesting bunch that seemed to desperately need new blood, which is why they did not hesitate to select me to run, with Jerry Plancher as my running mate. Together we would take on the two incumbent councilmembers, Sal Zisa and Bob Rathgeber, who were seeking to win their third term in office. Jerry had run for council a number of times but had never won. He was eager for a victory. To celebrate my being selected to run for office, Catherine and I went out for dinner. We joked about how the local organization's lack of enthusiasm and vigor was why they had not won in some time.

I hit the campaign trail running, hosting a fundraiser at my law office, sending out flyers about the issues in town, giving out pens and pads of paper with my name on them, and doing what I came to like and dislike most about campaigning, walking door to door for support. They call going to the homes of your constituents and asking what is most important to them and trying to garner their support "retail politics". The practice of this type of campaigning is time-consuming, but if you really want to immerse yourself in local issues, it's the best way to do it. And I did it better than anyone else in Ridgefield. I started walking the town after my selection as a candidate in April 1997 and continued right up until the day of the election in November.

On election night the tally showed that my running mate was soundly defeated, but Sal Zisa had edged me out by only single digits. My defeat was considered an upset because of how close the election results had been. After learning about the dubious nature of the many absentee ballots cast in favor of Zisa, I challenged the election and took the case to court. Unfortunately, it was in the Superior Court of New Jersey that I would eventually lose the election. Even though I demonstrated that many of the absentee votes were cast by people who no longer lived in town, the judge did not throw the ballots out, so I withdrew my challenge. I would run again in the next election rather than continue my court fight.

I learned a lot during my first election campaign, but two things really stood out. One was the massive time commitment that was necessary to run an effective campaign, even on a local level. The other thing was how nasty and vindictive political opponents can be when they see their power being threatened. A Republican councilman who knew that my family had a business in town had actually sent the building department official to investigate the location of a fence on the premises. The inspector found that the fence was millimeters over from where it should have been, so he fined and ordered my stepfather to take it down, even though the fence had been there for years. Once I entered politics, all bets were off. This is only one small example of what happened in Ridgefield if you went up against the party running the town.

In 1998, I searched for another running mate and found someone who grew up in town with me and was interested in the community. Jeff Trifari and I walked the town street by street almost every day and I raised money to get out our message. We attended every recreation, senior citizen, and church-oriented event we could.

That was also the year of the Clinton impeachment and trial before the Senate, where the president was not removed from office and the ramifications for Republicans were significant. In Ridgefield, residents were not happy with the way that Congress conducted themselves during the proceedings, and the prosperity Ridgefield residents enjoyed meant that many were happy with the president. As a result, the Democratic ticket in the general election of 1998 won in a landslide. Everyone on the Democratic side of the ballot won with significant margins, and I was the high vote getter of all of them. Despite the victories, the Democrats were still the minority party.

After the election Catherine and I decided that it was time to take a vacation, and in November 1999 we went on a two-week trip to England and France and had a great time sightseeing and spending some alone time together after such a hectic year. Neither of us had ever been to England or France, and we were making it a point to see as much of the world as we could before having children. Being a councilman-elect was a lot different than being just a council candidate, and once I was sworn into office I realized just how much responsibility and time went into performing the job properly. The municipal reorganization meeting took place during the first week of January, which is the law in New Jersey. These meetings were to officially establish the committees for the year, and prior to the meeting both Jeff and I were notified of the committees that we would be on. As expected, being the minority party, we were given very little responsibility. The important committees were reserved for the majority party, and Mayor Veale would never have given Jeff or me an olive branch by putting either of us on a major committee because he was very upset about losing the two council seats.

Jeff and I went about the year taking the positions we were given seriously, putting in a lot of effort on the job and hosting townwide meetings on issues that we saw as important for residents in the borough. We held a victory party and raised money for the campaign in 2000—which was going to be important since the mayor's seat was on the line, along with two council seats, meaning that if the Democrats took two of the three seats we would move to the majority party and be able to make the changes we believed in. I was asked and pressured to run for mayor, but did not think it was the right time. As a result, John Quaregna ran for the seat along with two candidates for council, and they were up against Mayor Veale, who was a formidable opponent and had not lost a municipal election in decades. Even at his advanced age, Veale was still very competitive and did not like to lose.

Mayor Veale's running mates were not that strong and when the results of the election came in that year, the Democrats managed to pick up one seat on the council. The council was split, and Mayor Veale became the tie-breaking vote. During the year 2000 that's just what he did, broke ties in favor of appointments and laws that we believed were not good ideas. Mayor Veale did not like a split council, and although he tried to adapt, things got worse for the Republicans in 2001. With Vice President Al Gore at the top of the ticket, the local Democrats in Ridgefield took the majority by winning both seats in the local race, which had been held by long-term Republicans.

The victory was significant as the Democrats had not been in the majority in Ridgefield in more than a decade. Jeff and I were now part of the new council majority, which included Bill Bonardi, the losing candidate from the prior year's election who was a lifelong resident, a newcomer to Ridgefield, Javier Acosta, who was from West New York and had lived in town for only a few years at that time, and Ed Catherina, who won the year before. We were excited about being able to make appointments in January and advance our agenda, replacing the Republican's outdated way of doing things.

In January 2001, the new council elected me council president, and New Jersey Superior Court Judge Mark M. Russello swore us all into office. The reorganization meeting took place on

January 3. At the meeting, the new Democratic majority made its first appointments in almost ten years. We were excited as we planned an ambitious agenda for the year: new facilities for our children, a new communications center for our emergency personnel, fulfilling our promises made during the last few years while campaigning, and trying to keep taxes flat, which was our number-one priority. One other thing—the Democratic majority did not reappoint municipal court judge Robert Avery, which led to some mean-spirited backlash in the fall when Jeff and I once again had to hit the streets campaigning.

We did not believe Judge Avery was doing a good job, and we had questions about his ethics. The judge was not happy about his not being reappointed and decided to run the Republican campaign against Jeff and me. Regardless of his efforts, we won by another large majority and continued to fulfill our agenda in town, which was moving the borough in the right direction. Other than some small personality issues, the Democrats on the council managed to work together and support one another in our elections until 2004.

In 2003, Mayor Veale did not seek reelection, and I ran for mayor. The mayoral campaign was very active, and in the end I won by a landslide, as did my entire ticket. We rented a campaign office, did polling, raised a lot of money to use in a fast-paced campaign, and celebrated at the annual New Jersey State League of Municipalities Conference in Atlantic City after we had won. Things were looking up until Jeff and Javier wanted a friend of theirs to fill my now vacant seat on the council while the other councilmembers had other people in mind. Jeff was also seeking the council presidency along with John Quaregna. These two issues did not resolve favorably for Jeff, and it ended up splitting the party for the next several years, which made campaigning more difficult than usual. Personal attacks worsened and were enhanced with the advent of the internet and online forums and blogs.

While I won my first mayoral campaign by almost one thousand votes, the divided party in 2007 resulted in my victory over Robert Avery by a little over one hundred votes. My two running mates lost, so I was the only Democrat on the Mayor and Council with six Republican councilmen who seemed to want nothing but to get me out of office, and to embarrass me along the way.

While going door to door during the course of one of my campaigns, I came upon a man who I had gone to high school with. Mike Mecca was a lifelong resident in town and from a very wealthy family. While I was going over my ideas and asking for his vote, I noticed that he appeared to be very bitter about a lot of things in town: the police, recreation, taxes. His complaints went well beyond the norm in terms of what the average resident would say to me at their doorstep. He seemed to have too much time on his hands and, as I found out later, wanted me out of office more than anyone I knew.

One morning in 2005, I received a call from a friend, Phil Ganci, who asked me if I was raiding the homes of residents in town. He had been reading the online blog nj.com and on the Ridgefield forum a resident had stated that his home was raided by me and that it was political in nature. I told Phil that I had never done that, it was a lie, and sought to stop the character assassination before it went too far. The poster was anonymous, so I had to file a lawsuit to obtain the identity of the person. I soon learned that the anonymous person was Mecca, and after protracted litigation, the defamation case was eventually dismissed because the judge who heard the matter did not believe that I suffered damages, even though he acknowledged that the statement was a lie. Mecca then sued me for malicious prosecution, which resulted in a jury verdict in my favor, but I still had huge legal bills.

When I brought the legal bills to the council's attention for reimbursement, explaining that the bills should have been covered by the borough, the council denied my request. By that time, due to Democratic infighting and poor campaigning over the past few years, the council had become a Republican majority again, and they were doing everything they could to hurt me personally. I likened them to the Taliban, since I believed they had declared war on me and my family. The council president was none other than Robert Avery, the former municipal court judge, and Mecca was a big supporter of my opponents.

Eventually, the town insurance carrier picked up the defense of my case, but I still had large legal bills prior to the coverage. A number of political officeholders recommended I set up a legal defense fund to raise money for the defense costs, because I was being treated unfairly. A friend advised me to hire Henry Klingeman, one of the state's best criminal defense attorneys who had set up these types of funds for other politicians and knew how things should be done legally. Little did I realize that this would lead me down a path that would change the direction of my life forever.

Chapter 3

MEETINGS WITH THE DEVIL

Ridgefield UNICO was a vibrant and well-respected charitable ethnic organization in the Borough of Ridgefield. You had to be Italian American or married to someone who was to belong. I joined the organization in 1997 after being a guest of my parents at a number of events that the organization had sponsored, from the annual Christmas dinner dance to the summer barbeque to the Brian Piccolo Awards dinner. I was able to reacquaint myself with people who I had known for years because I went to school with their children or knew them from my local parish, St. Matthew's.

Whenever UNICO had an event, there would be fundraising, and the money would be donated to a worthy cause or given to a Ridgefield Memorial High School student in the form of a scholarship. All of the members of UNICO were proud of their Italian heritage and regularly went to meetings and events because they enjoyed one another's company, loved to be reminded of their country of origin, and most importantly, because they wanted to help others. The long-time members of UNICO were always setting up the rooms, cooking food at the barbeques, and selling tickets for the many events that would take place during the year. These were the men who gave more than they received, and when an event went smoothly and everyone was happy, the Unicans had all that they wanted. One such man was Vincent Tabbachino.

Vinny Tab, as he was commonly known, was at every event with his wife Annette, working hard, helping others, and making people feel welcome. He would go out of his way to give you a hug and kiss your wife at every event. Vinny was the man who dressed up as Santa Claus during the annual Christmas tree lighting ceremony in town; he helped serve food to the handicapped during our annual UNICO Canteen; and he traveled around the country to represent Ridgefield UNICO at the many conventions that UNICO held during the course of the year. He was never in good physical condition, but when it came to UNICO, he always did more than his part.

Vinny's wife had gone to high school with my stepfather. Other than his involvement with UNICO, I did not know anything else about Vinny except that he seemed to be a successful business person who was involved in real estate, insurance, and preparing tax returns.

In early 2009, Vinny started calling me on my mayoral phone line listed in the phone book. He knew a prominent developer interested in doing some development in New Jersey. A guy named David Essenbach wanted to meet with me and discuss his potential plans for developing along the Overpeck Creek in town. This was significant because the council and I had been trying to get the property developed for nine years. One project after the other kept falling through, so when Vinny said that he knew someone who was interested in developing the area, I was enthusiastic to meet with him. It was a very busy time for me personally, but eventually I was able to meet Vinny and David at Patsy's in Fairview, a restaurant close to my Fort Lee law office that I frequented.

The position of mayor in Ridgefield, as in many small towns in New Jersey, is part-time even though the hours required make it literally a second full-time job. As mayor, it had been well within the norm to meet with various individuals at different times during the day related to town business.

Individuals who plan on spending millions of dollars on a real-estate project commonly feel the need to meet with leaders to ensure the project they are proposing is something that the town is looking for and willing to support. As the mayor, I was usually the individual that was contacted. As mentioned in the last chapter, Ridgefield's mayor-council form of government is a weak-mayor form, meaning that the council has virtually all the power. It effectively appoints all members of all boards, committees, and professionals, except the planning board, which is the mayor's appointment for the majority of the membership.

The planning board votes on large scale projects. If certain variances are required, however, then the zoning board is the body that makes the decision as to whether a project is going to be approved. At that time, the zoning board was appointed and run by my opponents on the council even though the planning board was made up of mostly my appointments.

I met with Vinny and David Essenbach on March 23, 2009, for lunch at Patsy's. When I arrived, it was an interesting sight to see. Vinny, an old-style Italian American, was sitting with an Orthodox Jewish man who wore a yarmulke and black-and-white clothing. Nevertheless, I spent about an hour talking to Vinny and David about the potential project. I explained what I would like to see on the site and what would benefit the town. David seemed to want a residential development that would require variances from the zoning board. I told him the zoning board was not under my control. Upon leaving the meeting, I told David that he should call the borough administrator or the planning board attorney, who could help him work through more of the specifics of the project and provide further information.

Vinny and I were left alone for a little while before I went back to work, and Vinny thanked me for taking the time to meet with David. He knew I had wanted to develop the area for a while and said that maybe David could do it because he was very interested. I reiterated the fact that he would have to go before the zoning board and get variances, since he stated that he wanted to build a residential development. I left the meeting thinking that I did what I would do for anyone who was interested in doing a development project in Ridgefield: I met with the developer and gave background information on what the town wanted. That is what any mayor would do under the circumstances, if he really cared about a project and the town that he represented.

Exactly four months later, on July 23, 2009, the world and I learned that David Essenbach was not really the developer that Vinny thought he was introducing me to. David was none other than Solomon Dwek, a serial fraudster who was now a cooperating witness with the FBI and the United States Attorney's Office.

It turns out Dwek was working with the government for almost three years on a two-track investigation into money laundering and political corruption and had entered into a cooperation agreement with the government in order to reduce the sentence he would eventually receive because of his past crimes. The irony is that to this day, I don't believe the government knew who they were dealing with and the laundry list of crimes that their cooperating witness had engaged in during his lifetime.

Born to a Syrian Jewish family, Dwek was a resident of Deal, a neighborhood in Ocean Township, New Jersey. He ran a real estate empire based on a pyramid scheme in and around Monmouth County under multiple business names, and was vice president of the Deal Yeshiva, (a nonprofit Orthodox Jewish religious school that his parents founded). The investors defrauded by Dwek were also members of the local Syrian Jewish community, including his uncle Joseph Dwek of Brooklyn, who was defrauded of $60.2 million. Dwek was well respected and trusted due to the reputation of his parents, who founded a yeshiva.

On October 20, 2009, Dwek pleaded guilty to federal bank fraud charges in US District Court in Newark, New Jersey, and later that day pleaded guilty to "misconduct by a corporate official." He was released on a $10 million bond until a scheduled prison sentencing date of February 9, 2010.

Dwek had agreed to act as an informant in Operation Bid Rig III in exchange for a lighter sentence. After Solomon Dwek's role as an informant became public, his father, Rabbi Issac Dwek, announced that his son Solomon was no longer welcome at his home and denounced the practice of acting as a government informant against other Jews.

Dwek was meeting with me as part of the political corruption investigation. To this day, I still find hard to believe that I was a target. I came to learn that Dwek and Vinny had laundered thousands of dollars between 2008 and 2009. Dwek had asked Vinny if he could introduce him to any politicians who would agree to take money in exchange for official action, in other words, people who were willing to sell their political office.

Although Vinny never actually told Dwek that I would engage in this type of activity, obviously he said enough to arouse Dwek's, and the government's, interest. That's when Dwek starting bugging Vinny to set up meetings with me. Since Vinny was being paid for any corrupt political officials that he could introduce to Dwek and since the investigation was coming to a close in spring 2009, Vinny was desperate to bring Dwek a politician as he had promised, and to keep the relationship going. He took advantage of his relationship with me through our UNICO connection and brought me to the table with Dwek under false pretenses. Vinny never told me that Dwek wanted to bribe me; he only said that Dwek was a ready, willing, and able developer who was interested in doing great things for Ridgefield.

Dwek recorded the meeting through a video and audio recording device, which we suspect was located on a button of his shirt. There were things I never noticed about the meeting at Patsy's with Vinny and Dwek until I reviewed the recordings over and over again. I could see Dwek manipulating the setting, moving things on the table in order to get a clear view of me for the camera.

Dwek would also make sure that he was sitting close to me so that he could get every word I said in hopes of implicating me in his scheme to have me commit a crime and thus reduce his sentence.

There was still nothing unusual with this type of meeting, except that I seemed to stick out like a sore thumb. Friends who viewed the tapes told me that when they watched them, it looked like I did not belong at the meeting. I was a mayor willing to fill in a supposed developer on a project that he seemed interested in taking on. Vinny and Dwek were money launderers and one was a government witness. They were unsettled and fidgety, and Dwek was always texting and using his phone. It was also strange that while Dwek purported to be a major developer, it seemed like he did not understand basic concepts of land use law as it pertained to the zoning and planning board. Dwek seemed to be somewhat clueless in this regard, because, as I later discovered, he wasn't listening to anything I was telling him.

The next month I left for Florida with my wife and children to go to Disney World, where we had planned on spending a relaxing vacation after winning the civil suit Mike Mecca had filed against me. It was a week-long trial where a jury awarded him no damages, finding that he had no cause of action based upon the facts of the case. I am still dumbfounded as to why the case was not dismissed for having no merit. It is hard to understand why the court held that Mecca had a constitutional right to lie about me.

By April, my whole family needed a vacation and my wife and I were looking forward to going to Florida and taking the kids to Disney. Sure enough, our luck had it that our daughter came down with a serious illness while we were at the resort, and we had to cut the vacation short by a number of days and flew home early.

Upon my return to Ridgefield, Vinny began frantically calling me at regular intervals to set up another meeting with Dwek. When we finally spoke, I asked him why he wanted to meet, since I had already sat down with Dwek. Vinny said that Dwek was going to acquire the properties and that it was important for him to explain to me what he was going to do in the area, but assured me that Dwek did not expect any promises or commitments. With that in mind, I had no problem sitting down with Dwek a second time, so we arranged to meet at Patsy's once again on May 18, 2009.

Both Vinny and I arrived early, and we spoke before Dwek arrived. Vinny told me that he was going to attend a cocktail party that had been scheduled as a fundraiser for my legal defense fund related to the Mecca case, and that he had spoken to David (Dwek) who wanted to attend. I told Vinny that was great but reminded him again that I could not make any promises or commitments to Dwek. Dwek showed up shortly thereafter.

Dwek arrived and after our greetings he started to talk about how his wife had just given birth to another son. Vinny congratulated him and then commented that the last time Vinny saw Dwek's wife she did not look pregnant. Dwek responded that she carries small. This was another Dwek lie. I later found out that Vinny and Dwek had gone out to eat with their respective spouses; however, Dwek was passing off an FBI agent as his wife. Vinny fell for it hook, line, and sinker. Dwek was the serial con man, and Vinny was the eager victim. Vinny never really had a chance.

We talked about our families, children, health problems, Atlantic City, and a big cellular antenna application that was being heard by the Ridgefield Zoning Board. Vinny then guided the topic toward the redevelopment project. I asked Dwek who he was dealing with at the company who owned the property, which was the old Pfister Chemical Company site. I also asked him about a neighboring property in the redevelopment zone. That's when Dwek started to double talk and confuse me as our discussion progressed. Dwek told me that he had been doing a project in Orange, New Jersey, and invested millions of dollars to buy the property. He said he was led to believe by the zoning board members that his hotel project would be approved for hundreds of rooms, but when the final decision was made by the board, he had to make significant changes, costing him thousands of dollars. Dwek said he ended up having a project approved for only a thirty- or forty-room hotel, and that he had to walk away from the project, losing all the money he had invested. Essentially, Dwek did not want to get screwed again like he did in "the Oranges."

Dwek kept saying that he did not want to have his project put on the bottom of the application pile. I kept telling him that there was no pile. The project was one that the town was trying to develop for the past ten years, and there were no applications for development. In fact, due to the lack of applications, in 2011 the zoning board was completely dissolved and combined with the planning board. When I was meeting with Dwek in 2009, there were simply no piles to be put on top of, and there was nothing to expedite his project like he asked. I told Dwek all of this at the meeting, but he seemed to ignore it whenever I told him, being more concerned about sending text messages and taking phone calls from his business associates, which I later learned was the FBI.

During the meeting I received phone calls from members of the planning board in town with regard to a cellular tower, which had been a major issue before the borough's zoning board of adjustment.

Whenever I would hang up, I did not have the chance to say much while Dwek was talking, since he would either roll onto another topic or speak over me. He seemed to be making a lot of assumptions in what he was saying, and I was not sure as to where he was going with the conversation. At one point, Dwek started to make some disturbing statements that left me thoroughly confused. He suggested that he could make a campaign donation to me even though I did not have an election coming up, or even a campaign account. He said he didn't want to have his name on anything, because he did not want any conflicts.

As the meeting drew to an end, I began to leave the table and was going to the men's room. I planned to go to my car immediately and then head back to the office. As I got up to shake Dwek's hand and wish him well, he hit me with a well-rehearsed script, hitting on different topics in rapid succession. He said he wanted to contribute money to my legal defense fund, told me not to put him on the bottom of the pile, and asked me to help him expedite his projects. These statements were confusing and troubling. Dwek kept talking over me, then headed for the exit door as George Michael's "Father Figure" played on the restaurant's music system.

After using the men's room, I left the restaurant. Vinny and Dwek were still in the parking lot. As I headed to my car, Vinny climbed into the passenger seat and said that Dwek had given him ten thousand dollars cash for my legal defense fund. Shocked, I refused to take the money, and then Vinny told me to take a check from him for ten grand. I told Vinny that I needed to talk to my lawyer before accepting the money. I was very troubled as I left the restaurant parking lot, wondering what had just happened.

On the way back to my office I called my wife and told her what happened. She confirmed that the meeting sounded odd. When I got back to my office, I arranged to have a meeting with my lawyer as soon as possible. When I met with my attorney Henry Klingeman, he confirmed that I was correct not to take the cash. He took the check that Vinny had written out and told me if I ever met with Dwek again that I should make it clear that I do business only in a legitimate and proper manner. Henry never told me to contact the authorities. If he had, I would have had no problem doing so.

About a week later, Vinny started again with his deluge of phone calls to set up yet another meeting with Dwek. I told him I would meet with Dwek again. As Henry had instructed, I wanted to make it clear to him that I play by the book. The last and final meeting with Dwek took place at Patsy's on May 28, 2009. Watching the recordings, you can see I was a man on a mission. As soon as Dwek arrived at the meeting, I began to explain to him—in between all of his text messages and phone calls—that I only do things legally and by the book. He would not hear anything of this and continued to speak over me. After coming back from the bathroom, Vinny even joined in to drown out what I was saying. After trying to make things clear to Dwek, I left the meeting intending to never again speak with him, meet with him, or have anything to do with him. I thought Dwek was crazy because of the nutty way he spoke and how he never listened to what I would tell him. I spoke with Vinny shortly after the meeting on the phone and told him I would not take the check from Dwek and that I wanted to send it back. Vinny told me to rip it up, but then convinced me to accept a check for twenty-five hundred dollars from him for my legal defense fund. He swore to me that it was not Dwek's money and that I would never have to meet with Dwek again. Vinny said that he felt bad for all he put me through and wanted to donate. That sounded good to me.

It turns out Vinny's word was no good. Over the next few weeks, I received numerous phone calls from Vinny, who wanted to set up yet another meeting with Dwek. The next time I saw Vinny was on July 23, 2009. He was sitting on a bench in the federal holding cell that I shared with him for the day. That is also when I would learn that David Essenbach was really Solomon Dwek, and most of my questions would be answered.

Chapter 4

SUMMER VACATION

Every summer since our daughter Laura was born, Catherine and I would rent a house on Long Beach Island for a week. We had been renting the same house on Eighty-fourth Street in Brighton Beach, only a couple of blocks from the beach, from 2002 until the summer of 2009. Year in and year out we had fantastic weather and Laura loved the trip. We usually would cap off our vacation with a visit to the Quaregnas, good friends of ours who owned a summer home in Manahawkin. We would take a cruise on their boat with Captain John Quaregna, or JQ as he liked to be called, at the helm.

John served on the Ridgefield Council with me for about four years, until he was defeated by an inferior challenger. Many attributed his loss to the media's campaign against him and the local Democratic ticket. The local rag for some reason had it out for the Ridgefield Democratic Organization, and it seemed like they never wrote a fair or balanced article about what we were doing in town. The paper liked sensational stories, and we joked that their motto was "Don't let the truth get in the way of a good story." That was the case when John ran for reelection in 2006. The paper decided that it should run front-page stories of work that John had done as a contractor in town (and claim it was done improperly) rather than run stories about those being killed in Iraq.

Although John and I met due to our mutual involvement in politics, our friendship continued after his tenure on the council ended, and we thought highly of one another's families. In fact, I always admired John's commitment to his family and how close-knit they were. Our annual barbecue and boat ride was the highlight of our Long Beach Island trip.

On July 18, 2009, Catherine and I were to begin our trek to Long Beach Island. We were going to be sharing the shore house with my parents, who had paid for the rental since they wanted to unwind with us after the stresses of the Mecca lawsuit. Little did we realize what the future held. As usual, I had overbooked my day. I had to perform a wedding in the morning and immediately afterward attend a press conference with Governor Corzine, who was promoting the Light Rail Train Line that was to have a stop in Ridgefield.

I had first met Governor Corzine when he was running for the United States Senate. Corzine had absolutely no political experience when he announced that he would seek the seat being vacated by Senator Frank Lautenberg, who was retiring from politics after serving for many years. What Corzine lacked in experience he made up for in something that all political parties could identify with in New Jersey: money. Corzine was the chairman of the board of directors for Goldman Sachs and was worth millions of dollars. Corzine easily could self-finance his campaign and donated money to every major Democratic political organization in the state of New Jersey to, in my view, buy his way to the nomination. He was being challenged in the primary election for Senate that year by former governor James Florio, and by spending his own money, Corzine beat Florio. During his campaign, he even managed to donate money to the Ridgefield Democratic Committee and came to some of our events that year. He then had a close battle with Congressman Bob Franks in the general election and was elected the state's junior senator, joining Senator Robert Torricelli in New Jersey's delegation to the United States Senate. Corzine was still serving his first term as senator when former governor James McGreevey resigned from the governorship due to a sordid sex scandal involving a man. When he resigned, the state senate president, Democrat Richard Codey, became the governor. Codey, who was very popular, could not challenge Corzine because of the money advantage that Corzine held.

Anyway, on the day I was to leave with my family for Long Beach Island, my schedule was full as usual. It was a hot and humid July morning in New Jersey, typical for that time of year. I put on a suit since I not only had to perform a wedding at Borough Hall, but I also had to meet up with Governor Corzine at the press conference. It was so hot and humid that my suit stuck to my body. When I arrived at Borough Hall there was a group of people waiting for me to perform the nuptials. As mayor, it was my job to perform civil weddings. I was always torn as to what I should wear to the weddings I officiated at Borough Hall. Most of the time, the couple showed up in casual clothing, and when I say casual I mean blue jeans or short sleeve shirts. Sometimes they wore shorts in the summer. Not to chance the one occasion that the couple arrived in formal clothing, I wore a suit every time I officiated a wedding. Sometimes I would wear a sports jacket, but I wore a tie no matter what. The prior mayor would don a robe that was also worn by the municipal judge to perform weddings. I always thought that was a bit tacky and decided to wear my own clothes. I also donated all of the proceeds from the weddings to the Ridgefield Youth Commission.

After performing the wedding at Borough Hall that morning, I got into my car and proceeded to the H&Y Marketplace, which was where the press conference was going to take place. H&Y was a new mall in town, and the owner was kind enough to allow the press conference to take place in the parking lot. A makeshift stop was set up where the train would pass through the area so that the politicians and other officials would have a place to stand and talk about the train line and how great this was for the area. In essence, everyone was taking credit for something that had been in the works for years, but it was most important for Governor Corzine to be able to stand at the rail and say he was pushing for the line since he was in a dogfight for reelection with Christie. Truth be told, after the press conference no one heard a word from Corzine about the project, and he lost reelection several months later. Corzine would have done anything to win reelection and despite his efforts, he lost by a landslide in November.

A group of politicians had gathered at the H&Y Mart for the press conference, including Assemblyman Gordon Johnson, Senator Loretta Weinberg, representatives from the Department of Transportation and New Jersey Transit, and a state trooper who was the advance man for the governor. The press was also there, from local to regional TV and print media. Everyone took their places once Corzine arrived, and he began to shake everyone's hands before taking his place at the podium at the start of the press conference.

As the host mayor I was asked to speak first, and then Corzine made his speech. He was never a good public speaker, and despite his years in the United States Senate and almost one full term as governor, his method was still awkward and uncomfortable. He always tried to be an everyman's politician, to project a "cool" image, but it didn't work. He always seemed to come across as a detached and aloof Wall Street millionaire who could not identify with the everyday people from New Jersey. (He was from Illinois.)

When the press conference was over, Hugo Jimenez, one of the candidates for election on the local Democratic ticket in Ridgefield, asked Corzine for help on his campaign. Corzine, always the schmoozer, said if it helps to have the governor walking the town going door to door with him, he would do it. Truth be told, after I was arrested on Thursday of that week, Corzine never came back to Ridgefield, and only mentioned the town when he spoke of my having to resign before my trial and said how he was exploring ways to take over the town. Based upon the way he was running Trenton, the Ridgefield residents were not happy with him, and it showed in the polls in the November election.

As Corzine left the press conference, I remember telling him that I thought that a great running mate for his campaign would be Senator Weinberg of Teaneck. This was the first election in New Jersey where the position of lieutenant governor would be on the ballot and the governor would be picking the candidate. The irony was that shortly thereafter, he chose Weinberg to be his running mate. The embarrassing part was that despite a Bergen County candidate on the ticket, he barely won the county.

Upon leaving the press conference, I went directly home and helped my wife finish packing for our trip. At last, rest and relaxation, and my whole family was looking forward to this annual excursion. The ride down the shore was uneventful, and the only difference was that we were going during prime summer season, which was the most expensive time to stay at the Jersey shore, but we were going as guests of my parents, so it didn't matter to us.

Growing up, my family had stayed in Beach Haven on Long Beach Island during the month of August every summer during my youth, and I wanted to continue that tradition with my own children. Catherine also loved the beach and had been going to the Jersey shore since she was a young girl. Her brother owned a house in Sea Girt, which is located to the north of Long Beach Island and is much more suburban than where we vacationed.

For those who do not know New Jersey, Long Beach Island is a strip of land to the east of the mainland connected by a single bridge. The island is only about ten miles long, and not very wide. In fact, during one of the worst storms to hit the island, the ocean actually met the bay. Long Beach Island is less than one mile wide at its widest point. You can see the bay from the beach at most points.

The house we rented every year was in a prime location on Brighton Beach. The ocean was only two blocks away, and there was a bike rental store, a take-out seafood restaurant, and a liquor store all within walking distance. We usually rented the first floor of the two-family house, since there was more room for our children and there was no danger of either of them falling from the top floor. Shore house rentals were empty homes and you had to bring everything from bedding and food to laundry detergent and toiletries. The price to rent was usually good for a family, but it was a vacation where you had to do all the cooking and cleaning. Since both our children suffered from severe food allergies, going out to eat was never really an enjoyable experience anyway, so this was the perfect vacation. We enjoyed going every year.

We arrived sometime in the early afternoon of July 18, 2009, and the weather was perfect as we unpacked our Toyota 4Runner. The truck was loaded with everything from sheets to pots and pans to food for the week. My parents followed with their car and we began to help them unload their items, which were not nearly as numerous as ours. Once the vehicles were unloaded, we put the food in the refrigerator, put the pots away in the kitchen cabinets, and made the beds.

Since it was such a nice day, we decided to hit the beach right away. Our children loved the beach, and it was such a pleasure watching them play in the sand and run into the water. Their enjoyment was often the best part of the trip.

We returned to the house around dinnertime, and the whole family ate a great home-cooked meal. It was often better than actually going out to a local restaurant, no crowds to deal with and we would be able to finish dinner, have some drinks, and play some games with the kids before they had to go to sleep.

Essentially the whole week down the shore was the same routine every day. I would get up early in the morning, usually before everyone else in the house. Careful not to wake anyone, I would go to the back yard, quietly unchain my bicycle, and take a ride for about an hour down to Beach Haven. The route was always the same, and I would always listen to music during this time. I would get back around eight or nine in the morning. By then everyone was just getting up, and we would eat breakfast together. Then we would get ready for the beach: applying suntan lotion, putting on bathing suites, and packing up the beach bags and equipment so that we could carry all of the items to the beach that would preoccupy the kids for the day. There were lots of beach toys, shovels, kites, books, and bottles of water.

We would usually stay at the beach until the early afternoon before heading back to the house for lunch, which would either be a sandwich or hamburger, and then we'd go back to the beach, where we'd left our umbrella and towels, and remain there until about six o'clock, which was usually a perfect time when the beach cleared out and you could really enjoy the sounds of the surf and watch the kids play in the water or make sandcastles. After that we would go home for dinner, play games with the kids, watch television with the adults, and everyone would go to bed early. We would get up the next day and do it all over again. This was the way we would spend our week down at the shore, and it was always the perfect vacation. The only difference would be that on certain evenings we would take the kids out for some ice cream or on the Friday night before we left we would go to Fantasy Island, which was an amusement park not far from the beach house. We'd pay one price for the kids to go on every single ride they could possibly go on in a few hours.

This was the way we would spend every vacation down the shore, every year since 2002, at least until this summer of 2009. I still vividly remember the evening of July 22, 2009. Catherine and I walked to the beach with the kids after dinner, and we watched them enjoy running on the sand as we sat on beach chairs. We both noticed how incredibly peaceful the vacation had been and how great the evening was for both of us and the kids. Life was great, and it seemed like we did not have a care in the world. We went home with the kids when it got dark and went to bed early that night. Not one for ever having a good night's sleep, it was ironic that that night I slept soundly. That is until my usual time to go for my morning bike ride on that fateful day of July 23, 2009.

Chapter 5

HANGING WITH THE RABBIS

hortly before noon on July 23, 2009, I was processed at a federal building I had passed thousands of times in my life but had no idea that it housed the local Newark office of the FBI. A number of rabbis who were arrested that morning, some other handcuffed individuals, and I were led to a bus. We were subjected to a "perp walk" in which the agents made sure the press corps from all over the tri state area could get as many pictures of us as possible. On the bus we were told to have a seat. The FBI agent who was escorting me smiled for a couple more pictures before sitting down next to me. Naturally, the pictures would show up in every form of media possible, including in my opponents' campaign flyers that were sent out in that year's election and every election following 2009.

The bus took a short route to the federal courthouse, through a narrow passageway reserved for authorized vehicles, and down to the back of the building. Still in shock and disbelief, I do not remember saying anything to anyone on the bus. The FBI agent who was next to me seemed to be waiting for me to say something incriminating that she could use against me. Not only did I have nothing to say, I was still so confused I could not speak even if I had felt like talking.

When we left the bus and began to walk down the driveway into the federal courthouse, I distinctly remember the FBI agent telling me that I would now be in the custody of the United States Marshal's office, and that they would not treat me as well as I was being treated in the FBI office. I did not pay much attention, since I did not think that I was being treated all that well in the FBI office anyway.

When I entered the federal courthouse, a building that I'd visited on a number of occasions for my clients, we were in the basement. I had never been in the basement. That was where they held the prisoners. I was then escorted into a holding cell where I saw Dennis Elwell, the mayor of Secaucus, sitting on a bench. He nodded at me and put his head down. Vinny Tabbachino was sitting next to Elwell. Vinny noticed me as soon as I walked into the cell and shouted to the entire room at the top of his lungs, "What is this guy doing here? He didn't do anything except have lunch with the guy!" I looked at Vinny, sat down next to him, and told him to shut up.

After sitting next to Vinny for about two hours and hearing all the small talk, I noticed something odd. There were a lot of rabbis and politicians in the confines of the cell. Other than Vinny and Elwell, I did not know anyone else, which was to my detriment as the others began to think that I was a plant and began to ask me questions. I did not feel like talking, which made me seem even more suspicious.

After a couple hours, they took me from the cell and brought me to another holding area where I was told to strip down and was searched by the members of the United States Marshal's Service, another humiliating experience that I had to endure on the worst day of my life. After being strip searched, I was brought to the hallway and told to face the wall, where I was shackled from my feet and hands and told not to look anywhere else but forward. I was then led into a room where I was processed by the Marshal's Service. They asked me a number of questions before leading me back to the jail cell. In a cell across from the one I had shared with the rabbis, politicians, and Vinny, some not too friendly looking inmates yelled at me as I passed. I was concerned about what was going to happen next. I certainly didn't want to be placed in the cell across the way, but I felt like I was going to hit someone in my cell because people continued to try to speak with me. I was hungry and on edge. We were never offered anything to eat, despite the fact that we were in jail all day. It really didn't matter because I did not want to eat prison food anyway. So I just sat and waited for what would happen next.

After another long period of time, about four hours, we were all taken into the hallway, brought into an elevator, and then to another holding cell upstairs, which adjoined the courtroom where I would have to make my first appearance before Magistrate Madeline Cox Arleo. Before that day, I never knew a holding cell adjoined the courtroom. I can still hear the marshal say at some point that we were the best-behaved individuals he ever had to deal with. I was now in a smaller cell with a bunch of rabbis and politicians. It was the calm before the storm. One of the rabbis said his afternoon prayers before we were taken out into the courtroom. Vinny, a diabetic, was about to pass out because of his blood sugar. They still hadn't give us any food all day, despite his medical condition, so the marshal gave Vinny a piece of candy. We did not have to wait much longer, as the door opened and we were led out into the media circus.

There were a number of United States Attorneys at the prosecution's table, and a lot of press behind them. The ankle irons were cumbersome and I almost tripped walking up the stairs to the jury box, which is where we were all supposed to sit. As I walked up to the last row of seats and made my way down to the end of the row, I looked out into the audience and saw one friendly face among the crowd. My stepfather, who had been waiting for me all day was there, smiling at me as if to say that everything was going to be all right.

After I was seated, Henry Klingeman, my attorney at that time, came through the crowd and gave me a copy of the criminal complaint that had been filed against me. It turns out I was caught up in the third phase of Operation Bid Rig, the biggest undercover sting in New Jersey history. It began in 2002 when former Ocean Township Mayor Terrance D. Weldon pled guilty to extortion. He took bribes from developers to approve their building projects. The second phase of the investigation took place in 2003-04. Investigators set up a shell company. Developer Robert "Duke" Steffer solicited public officials for projects. The investigation snared more than twelve public officials. The third phase of the investigation—Operation Bid Rig III—began after Dwek was arrested for committing $50 million in bank fraud, became a cooperating witness for the FBI, and agreed to infiltrate a money-laundering network in Brooklyn and New Jersey. The network had allegedly laundered tens of millions of dollars through charitable nonprofit organizations controlled by rabbis in New York and New Jersey. Dwek went after rabbis, public officials, and mayoral and council candidates. Henry told me to waive the probable cause hearing because I did not want to get indicted at that time. I flipped through the complaint while the court session continued for the others. I could not believe what I was reading. It seemed that a criminal case was being laid out against me with only statements that were made by Vincent Tabbachino to the government's confidential witness, Solomon Dwek.

Yes, I had met with Dwek on three occasions, but I never promised him anything, never took his money, and as I maintained right to the end, never did anything wrong. What was the government thinking? How could they prosecute an innocent man? Did they not care that I clearly told this person that I only act legally and that I did not take his money? Obviously not, but I sure hoped that I could convince someone that this was a big mistake and that the case should be dropped. Vinny was also saying all day long that he would make sure that I was cleared since he was the one that got me into this mess.

Eventually I was released from the courtroom after I said that I would waive the probable cause hearing and went into the room next door to fill out some paperwork outlining the conditions of my release. Next, I had to go to the pretrial office on the first floor. There, I met with a pretrial officer who told me I needed to call her once a week and meet with her once a month. I also had to inform her of any changes in my employment or address and let her know if I had any run-ins with the law. The officer would visit my home within the next few weeks, which was a humiliating experience, as she made sure that my family knew we were criminals and that big brother was indeed now watching us.

After giving a urine test that the feds ask if you would consent to but don't tell you it's not required, I left the federal courthouse with my stepdad, and the sea of photographers and news media moved in on us. It had started to rain, so we raced out of there in opposite directions. The media followed my stepdad, which ended up being a good strategy since he was on the evening news and not me. We met at the parking lot outside Henry's office and left Newark for the long ride back to Long Beach Island.

The ride back to the vacation house is a blur. I remember thinking: Why me? Is this really happening? How could the feds have gotten it so wrong? When will this be over so me and my family can be free to enjoy our lives?

We drove up to the house in Long Beach Island around six o'clock p.m., the time when we would normally be leaving the beach to come back home for dinner and begin to play games with the kids and then put them to bed. That evening when I entered the house, I could see my wife and mother had been crying. I told them not to worry about me since everything was going to be all right. The kids were in the back of the house playing. They didn't know what was going on. It was good to be back and see everyone again, but naturally I could not focus on anything for the rest of the night, not even the dinner my mother had made for me while we were gone. I don't remember what else I did that night, or even going to bed, but we must have somehow gone to sleep because the next morning, Friday, we were up and trying to enjoy the last day of our vacation of summer 2009.

We went to Fantasy Island with the kids, and I felt paranoid that everyone was looking at me, like they knew who I was and were wondering what I was doing there. When we returned to the vacation house that afternoon, the owner who had rented the home to us was acting strange. He obviously knew what had happened. I had to get used to this awkward feeling, as many people began acting in a strange manner when they saw me after July 23, 2009.

At the end of the day, we packed up our belongings and loaded them onto the truck, since we had to leave early Saturday. The plan was to head back to Ridgefield right away, but my partner at work, Jay Yacker, had a shore house in Harvey Cedars that he was not using that weekend. He wanted me to stay down the shore for a little longer so that the media attention could blow over. I gladly accepted his invitation, grateful for the opportunity to relax a little longer and make up the lost vacation days.

The Yacker family vacation home was fantastic. They had the second floor of a duplex house that was right on the bay. There was a Jacuzzi in the back, and it was walking distance to the beach. We stayed there until Sunday night and made the most of our extra time. During the weekend, friends had been constantly calling to see how I was, and I even had a friend visit me to see how the family was doing during this trying time. I was also in communication with a number of friends who were lawyers, able to make recommendations of white-collar criminal defense attorneys to me. I even set up a meeting with one of them on the Sunday evening that I returned from my trip.

I also received the first of a number of phone calls and messages calling for my resignation. The first was from Mike Kasparian, the Bergen County Democratic Chairman, the leading political Democratic county official. Kasparian had just come into power after his predecessor had been indicted. He never had a relationship with me and did not even have the nerve to speak with me one on one; instead, he cowardly left a message on my phone's voicemail saying I should do the right thing and resign. How was resigning the right thing when I was an innocent man? What type of message would that send to others? Do we really want to give that much power to prosecutors? Should they be able to accuse any politician of a crime and force them to leave office? I would not resign. In fact, I ended up holding office longer than Kasparian did, since he resigned and did not make any positive impact on the Bergen County Democratic Party during his tenure.

My one joke about Kasparian is that he called me three times in my life: the first time to ask me to support him to become the Democratic Chairman, the second time to tell me I should resign, and the third time, after I had been acquitted, to tell me that I could do anything I wanted with my life. Needless to say, I did not resign.

On Sunday night we packed up the truck and headed home, wondering what the future was going to hold for us as we made our way north up the Garden State Parkway. When we reached Ridgefield, I dropped off the family and left for my law office in Fort Lee. I had scheduled a meeting with my good friend Eric Harrison, who is one of the best civil trial attorneys I know, and an attorney he recommended for my defense.

Ten years earlier, Eric represented Ridgefield in a lawsuit brought by two police officers who were fired for allegedly engaging in abuse of office. I did not have much contact with him at that time, but the second time he represented the town, in a handicap discrimination case, I had much more interaction with Eric and saw that he was a great attorney. I was the only elected official to testify in court, and Eric prepared me to testify. When I saw him in action in the federal courthouse, I was convinced he was one of the best civil attorneys in the state of New Jersey. His subsequent defense of me in the Mike Mecca case solidified my opinion of him, and we had grown to become good friends. I respected his opinion. Eric did not know the attorney I was meeting, but one of his partners said that I should retain him since he was the best white-collar defense attorney in the state.

Meeting with a criminal attorney and Eric in my office was not a great way to spend a Sunday night, but it was important for me to get my ducks in a row and have a defense attorney ready for the battle I faced. We went over the case for over two hours. In the end, we decided that I had to go to the Mayor and Council meeting the next night. There were only two Mayor and Council meetings a month and that Monday happened to be the fourth Monday in July. I had to face the public. Missing a meeting would show that I could not do my job and bolster the case for those calling on me to resign. This attorney would show up to the Mayor and Council meeting on Monday night to lend me assistance. Thereafter I would probably retain him. I was dreading the Mayor and Council meeting on Monday night, but it was now a necessary evil. I had to go to the meeting.

When I woke up Monday morning, I could not believe the amount of press that was outside my little Cape Cod home in Ridgefield. I could not remember that many members of the press in town in all my life. Now they were descending on my block, taking pictures of me taking out the garbage and the recycling, leaving in the morning for work, arriving at town hall, and arriving at my place of business in Fort Lee. The press would camp outside my office, waiting to get a glimpse of me as I entered in the morning and left at night.

My experience with the press had never been great. I always had a low opinion of the reporters for my town, especially the local newspaper. However, the way the press treated me and my family throughout this experience would solidify my disrespect of the news media. The papers not only had me pegged as guilty from day one, there were constantly running articles and editorials of things that were inaccurate, misleading, or just plain untrue. We have a saying about the press in Ridgefield: they don't let the facts get in the way of a good story. As though their stalking me was not bad enough, one day a reporter showed up at my daughter's day camp in August 2009 and was told to leave.

One of the best things that came out of all this was the reception I got from the members of my community who sent me well wishes through email and letters to my home. Those sentiments offset the nasty news coverage and kept me and my family going through the tough times we faced.

Chapter 6

GUILTY UNTIL PROVEN INNOCENT

During everything that happened to me, the thing that members of the press and even members of my own political party forgot was that we are all innocent until proven guilty. Even though I am a civil attorney and never tried a criminal case in my entire career as a lawyer, I learned this basic concept in law school, and even remember learning it back in high school. Unfortunately, many people quite simply forgot the concept or threw it aside in a rush to judgment.

From the day that I received the phone call from Democratic County Chairman Mike Kasparian, the onslaught of those calling for me to resign was constant. The most notorious was former governor Jon Corzine. The same man who had visited my town the Saturday before I was arrested, supporting me and the local Democratic party, now wanted me and every politician charged on July 23 to resign from office as soon as possible.

Democrat Corzine was clearly concerned about his reelection campaign. He knew he faced Republican Chris Christie, the former United States Attorney who made political corruption the focus of his tenure as United States Attorney and, now, a part of his campaign theme, and he didn't want to be outdone by Christie when it came to ferreting out corruption. Christie knew his days were numbered after the election of 2008, since President Obama would never appoint him for another term. Christie left the United States Attorney's Office to run for governor while the Dwek sting was in full swing. The plan, in my mind, was clear: Christie left it to his underlings to continue the operation, which would target primarily Democratic bastions and help him take the governor's seat, since the arrests would take place during the heat of the gubernatorial election. The voting public would never suspect that Christie had anything to do with the sting since he was not in charge when the takedown occurred, but many high-ranking members of the United States Attorney's Office assisting in the sting would be rewarded with jobs in the new Christie administration.

After the arrests in July 2009, Corzine immediately called for everyone arrested and holding public office to resign. The facts of each case did not matter. If you were charged, you had to resign. It did not matter that we lived in the United States of America, and we were presumed innocent. Everyone had to resign. It did not matter if lives were being destroyed by false charges, or how innocent some of us were. We had to resign.

Many people thought that Corzine was a hypocrite, and it blew up on him in November. His overwhelming lack of popularity and tepid support among even Democrats caused Corzine to get smashed at the polls, and he took down a number of prominent Democrats who were also up for election on his ticket.

Several years earlier, Newark mayor Sharpe James, who was also a state senator, was indicted for political corruption. Corzine was the governor then and never demanded that James resign. Now Corzine was demanding that everyone who was arrested, before being indicted, resign from office. As far as I was concerned this was total nonsense, and I would never resign my office. Such a request coming from a man of Corzine's questionable character emboldened me even more to remain in office. In fact, I held my office longer than Corzine did as he lost his reelection bid in 2009 and was later investigated for actions he engaged in as CEO of a Wall Street equity firm after being thrown out of office.

Of the three mayors who were arrested—Peter Cammarano from Hoboken, Dennis Elwell of Secaucus, and me—I was the only one who stayed in office, despite Corzine's calls for me to resign. In fact, Corzine went so far as to unleash the office of the state comptroller, an investigative body for governmental fraud and abuse, on the borough to investigate any illicit activity. Little did Corzine realize that Ridgefield has a weak mayor and strong council form of government and was being run by my opponents for the past several years. Corzine's actions adversely affected only my opponents and their appointments. It was amusing in and of itself, but what was not funny was Corzine's decision to freeze all development applications for the borough until they were reviewed by a state agency. All applications before the zoning board, planning board, and the building department, after being approved in town had to be sent to Trenton for final approval. This was not only cumbersome, but unnecessary. Essentially, this was Corzine's way of showing the voters of New Jersey that he wouldn't stand for even a hint of corruption in government. Corzine's polling numbers were down and, in my opinion, he would push anyone out of office and throw anyone under the bus to save his own campaign. Eventually, he looked like a bully from Trenton who was throwing a temper tantrum, and I believe it came back to bite him and assist him in his loss of record proportions. The way things ran on Wall Street, where he came from, was much different than New Jersey politics. In reality, it was out-of-control property taxes, which were killing all New Jersey residents, that caused Corzine to lose. He also had no backbone and failed to generate any movement to get his base out to vote for him on election day.

It seemed that Corzine's calls for me to resign were in the paper every day. He allowed the issue to become a distraction to his campaign, so much so that he was contemplating a state takeover of the borough. He even sent his "ambassadors" to Bergen County to meet with me and to convince me to resign. If I resigned, he would say I did the right thing and wish me good luck in my efforts. My response to the papers and to Corzine was always the same, "Why would I resign if I did nothing wrong?"

The newspapers jumped on the bandwagon, saying that the upcoming trial was going to be a distraction to me, that I would not be able to focus on running the town, and that I had to go. However, the newspapers knew that I was one of many mayors in New Jersey who were able to do the job while holding down full-time employment, since the majority of mayors were part time. The local media knew that Ridgefield was a borough form of government. Essentially, the council ran the town, made the appointments, and had an administrator, who the Council hired, to run the day-to-day operations of the town. The only thing I could do, and had been doing since 2007, was chair the two Mayor and Council meetings per month, perform weddings, and appoint some members to the planning board. The local media had to know that the upcoming trial would not interfere with my mayoral duties, which did not take up a lot of time, and meetings took place in the evenings. Corzine, however, did not know how a municipal government ran, since he never held local office and bought his way into the United States Senate.

Most disappointing were the public calls for resignation by two women who had been friends of mine throughout my political career. Assemblywomen Joan Voss truly felt horrible for what had happened and for what I was going through. The state party pressured her to call for my resignation. Joan called me regularly, and I called her to find out what was going on in the state and why Corzine was taking the stance for me to resign. She would frequently ask me, "Were you set up?" I did not know how to respond other than to tell her that all of the evidence would eventually come out at trial. She also told me in private not to resign.

Assemblywoman Connie Wagner was a different story. She never called me, asked how I was doing, or sought to see how my family was being affected. She was scared of her own shadow and my problems were not good for her campaign, so she stayed away from me. She even sponsored some meaningless anti-corruption legislation during this time to show the voters she was tough on crime because she was also up for reelection in the fall. She was not a real friend.

Ironically, one of the individuals who was running against Voss and Wagner in the fall election of 2009 was Ridgefield council president Nicholas Lonzisero, who was regularly calling for me to resign. Lonzisero is a local Ridgefield guy who is a few years younger than me, but looks at least five years older. He is a multimillionaire bachelor who inherited his fortune from his family's real estate business.

Essentially, Lonzisero collected rent money for a living. He drove around town in his brand-new Mercedes Benz, or another new car—he bought a new one every year. He is not a likeable person, and his first move after he won election in 2007 was to attempt to evict me from the mayor's office in town hall. The office had been used by all mayors prior to my tenure since the building had been built. Every councilman, including me, respected the space even though the prior mayor was a Republican. But true to form, Lonzisero couldn't care less about the office, and only cared about advancing his own interests. The idea blew up in his face as the news media zeroed in on the issue and made him look like a fool, so he was forced to retreat on the issue, which made him and the rest of the council look foolish. Nevertheless, Lonzisero, along with his Republican councilmates, would make removing me from the mayor's seat the focus of their remaining years in office.

The media was consistently trashing me on television and the local paper took any shot it could at me, either through a news story—no matter how factually inaccurate it may have been—or an editorial about how I should no longer be in office. Political office holders, both Republican and Democrat, were also asking me to resign, and on top of this, I was concerned about how I was going to pay the bills.

Although the job of mayor in Ridgefield was part time, I regularly put in way more than thirty hours a week. Since the job paid less than eight thousand dollars per year, I relied on my full-time day job as an attorney to pay the bills. Neither Catherine nor I were independently wealthy, so we needed to have a source of income to support our two children and ourselves. I had been the sole breadwinner in the family since our oldest child, Laura, was born, and had maintained a very busy law practice.

The law firm that I had worked at since 2003 was owned by Ron Dario, who I knew since I finished my clerkship after law school. We had worked together at a small litigation firm for a number of years when I decided to leave for a much larger firm in 1998. It was there that I learned a great deal about working for corporate clients and insurance companies and continued to grow my private practice. There I was also able to work with Patrick Papalia, a very good attorney and even better friend. I mention their names since they supported me and my family throughout our ordeal.

Ron never entertained the idea of letting me go, despite great pressure from the outside. Most of the attorneys we dealt with were also very supportive of me and always asked him how I was doing whenever he would see them in court or at various legal proceedings. Had I not been able to work, I would not have been able to pay the bills, like most of the other people who were arrested on that fateful day. It was because of the support of friends like Ron and Pat that I was able to fight the charges against me to the end. In fact, on the day that I was arrested and interviewed by a woman at the Federal Building while she put together my dossier for bail conditions, one of the questions she asked me was whether I was still going to be employed at my current job after that day. I emphatically said yes, and she appeared puzzled.

My law practice, which had been built up over almost twenty years, consisted of many private clients, along with a number of public ones sprinkled in between. My main public jobs were township attorney for the township of Saddle Brook, rent control board attorney for the town of West New York, rent board attorney for the borough of Dumont, and ethics board attorney for the borough of Fort Lee.

With the onslaught of bad press and the pressure on municipalities to fire anyone who was charged with a crime on July 23, the public jobs came to an end. The borough attorney for Dumont called me within a week and asked me to submit a resignation letter or else I would be terminated. I never got that job back despite being found innocent and reapplying years later. Sal Vega, the mayor of West New York, did not even call me. He sent me a certified letter terminating me. I eventually would get that job back, but only after the mayor lost reelection and his opponent rehired me. The mayor of Fort Lee had the decency to contact me directly and let me know that I would have to resign, but would get the job back once I was cleared of all charges.

The one job that I never actually lost was the township attorney for Saddle Brook. The mayor of the Township, Louis D'Arminio, kept my firm on until I was cleared of all charges. Once that occurred, he reinstituted me as the township attorney. I will always be grateful to Mayor D'Arminio and the council, who never lost faith in my innocence. In fact, Mayor D'Arminio always told people the story of how we were at a convention in Atlantic City and a vendor offered dollar chips to all mayors at one of the casinos. He remembered how I would not even take the one-dollar chip, and how other mayors were unhappy with the way I turned down the nominal gift, even though it was legal to receive such an item. He was a former police sergeant and knew criminal law. He would consistently ask me how the federal prosecutor could have brought such charges against me when I never promised the government's witness a thing and never took any bribe. I would agree and move onto another topic, since it was too painful to discuss at times.

With the loss of all the public jobs, I took a massive salary hit, but was still able to get to the end of the trial without going into debt by drawing down on our family savings for our future and the future of our children. If this wasn't a good investment in our future, I didn't know what else was.

The one thing that would consistently disappoint me throughout the next year was the way certain members or organizations in the legal profession would treat me. Even though the United States Constitution declares an indicted person innocent until proven guilty, many professionals treated me as though I were already guilty. For example, I had been a member of the Attorney Fee Arbitration Committee in Bergen County for several years. I was appointed to that position by the New Jersey Supreme Court. It entailed a meeting approximately once a month, wherein panelists would meet with an aggrieved client and their former attorney and decide whether or not the client was overbilled for services. It was a volunteer position that satisfied my pro bono requirement for the New Jersey State Bar, and I actually enjoyed it. Shortly after my arrest, I was contacted by the chairwoman of the committee. To my surprise, she informed me that I would no longer be on the committee. Here was a legal committee that should honor the precept of innocent until proven guilty, but, just like in political circles, it seemed that I was presumed guilty.

I resigned from the committee and was actually able to focus more time and attention on my clients, family, and the next step in the process that I had to face. I realized more and more that you had to prove your innocence. You see, in New Jersey, when you are a public official charged with a crime, you are presumed guilty.

Chapter 7

MEDIA CIRCUS

Monday, July 27, 2009 was my first day back to work following my arrest. When I left my house, the morning circus commenced. That is, the press corps was camped outside my home waiting to get a photo of me at my worst. Of course, they would make sure that any photo of me to make the paper or their website would be the worst that they could find; me taking out the garbage from the house or carrying my briefcase with some strange look on my face. Some of the photographers apologized, and I understood that they were just doing their job. It was the editors of the newspaper who were the mean-spirited ones that ran with the most unflattering photographs to lead the story.

My morning ritual was to get into my car in the driveway, leave the house while the photographers followed, and get to my office in Fort Lee, which was about ten minutes away without traffic. I would then be surrounded by the press while I entered the building to start my day.

On that first Monday back, when I got to the office I noticed a news van camped out in front of the office waiting to harass me before I checked into work. Seeing the media frenzy in front of the building where I usually parked, I headed to the secure rear lot of the building where the press would not be able to enter. Coming in through the rear of the building I noticed the building employees who had always enjoyed a cordial relationship with me. One of the doormen was from Haiti, and every day as I would see him in the building, when I came through the front entrance or when he dropped off the office mail, he went out of his way to speak with me about politics in his home country. That morning he told me how the scene reminded him of a third-world political coup. He also told me how he knew the charges were false and how I would get through this mess and come out on top. I appreciated my talks with him. He was one of the people I never noticed in my everyday travels but was there to show support for me during my darkest days.

That morning I tried to get some work done since I had been out of the office for what seemed like an eternity. Normally, the month of July is a slow time of year for me and the perfect time to take a vacation. When I sat down and opened up my email, I noticed a large amount of unopened mail from senders that I did not recognize. Almost all of them were from people who I had not spoken with for a long period of time. They wished me the best for my future, declaring that they knew I was innocent and that this would all be behind me one day in the near future.

I then began to go through my snail mail, and again there were letters from people in Ridgefield or those who had moved out of town, writing to wish me their best, to let me know that they were praying for me and my family. I also received a number of prayer cards and other religious paraphernalia, which I came to treasure during the times when I felt alone. I knew there were many people praying for me.

After going through the motions of my first day back from vacation and trying to pretend that the weight of the world was not on my shoulders, I engaged in what would become my morning ritual until the day of my trial in October 2010. I checked in with my partner and friend Shelley Albert in the office next to mine. She became a real sister to me during this crisis.

Shelley is a former assistant district attorney for New York County, and is one of the smartest attorneys that I know. She also is a good friend and would meet with me in her office every morning for about an hour. We would talk about what was going on in my case and how I was going to get this behind me. As a former prosecutor, she was shocked that this case was even proceeding at all. Every time we spoke she would grow angry over the case, and she became even more upset as we came to know more and more about the confidential informant, Solomon Dwek.

I would usually start the conversation with Shelley by asking how this could be going on, and she would hash out various theories and ideas that she had. That Monday she recommended I speak with a white-collar defense attorney from her former office, who was an associate at the office of Benjamin Brafman, a high-profile criminal defense attorney from New York City who came to represent some of the Rabbis involved in the sting.

By midday, things had not let up at all. I could not even leave the office at lunchtime since the media was outside to harass me, so I ordered in. My office was on the first floor and had a view of the front of the building. Every time I looked out the window, I could see the news van. They refused to leave without an interview. I thought to myself, "Isn't there any other newsworthy events for them to cover? How interesting could I really be?" It seemed that this ritual carried on throughout the entire summer, with the cameras, reporters, and phone calls coming at me all day long.

The media phone calls were the other harassing aspect of what I had to deal with during the day. All day long I would get phone calls on my cell phone from strange numbers. Television stations, newspapers, and radio stations were trying to get an exclusive interview of me. Eventually, I stopped taking calls from the phone numbers that I could not identify. The press was ruthless.

One aggressive young reporter really seemed to cross the line both with how far he went to try to get an interview and with how strictly he adhered to not letting the facts get in the way of a good story. He left a message on my cell phone while I was still down the shore on vacation during the weekend of July 23 saying he wanted to interview me about my arrest. Naturally, I never returned his phone call. Not to be deterred, he got friends of mine to provide him with the address of our vacation house. I could not believe that someone would stoop so low as to track me down on vacation with my family during the worst time of my life to get a story. But that is the nature of the beast known as the press corps.

As the workday came to a close, the Mayor and Council meeting was drawing nearer, and I began to imagine what it was going to be like. I never could have guessed how crazy things were about to get. The defense attorney that I met through Eric Harrison, who was dying to get me to retain him as my attorney for the case, attended the Mayor and Council meeting to see the lay of the land. The meeting started early, at 5:30 p.m., because we had a work session, which was a meeting before the public meeting where the governing body would discuss matters and laws that were contemplated for action in the near future. The early evening start time was inconvenient for those of us on the council who had regular day jobs, unlike people like council president and assembly candidate Nicholas Lonzisero. Unfortunately, Lonzisero's people were in the majority, and I had to abide by their schedule. Rather than giving him the satisfaction of seeing me miss a meeting, I not only attended every work session, I was never late.

At about 4:30, I left work and met defense counsel Kevin Marino at my house before the press had assembled. We left together in his car and grabbed a slice of pizza before the meeting. We strategized a game plan for the evening. Kevin reviewed and revised a statement I had prepared, which I was to read at the beginning of the meeting, and we discussed how I would handle myself during and after the meeting. Before we left, one of my DPW workers came up to me and assured me that he knew I was innocent because I wouldn't be stupid enough to throw away my life for $10,000. I told him that I wouldn't throw my life away for any amount of money.

The community center was where we had been conducting the Mayor and Council meetings for the past several years. Borough Hall was not handicap compliant and the building was the subject of a number of lawsuits over the years, so I had decided that the best way to avert any and all future lawsuits against the town was to hold meetings at the community center, which was a handicap compliant building. The parking lot was packed even though hardly any members of the public ever attended a work session, no less one in the middle of the summer. Obviously, people were there to see how I would act after the big take down.

As I exited the car a number of people, young and old, that I knew from town, made their way toward me to wish me well. People say that the job of mayor is a thankless one, but that has never been my experience. A young woman that I knew only in passing, a staunch Republican no less, rode up with her son on a bicycle just to let me know her family supported me. A senior citizen who I knew from town approached me, crying, and hugged me and said that she was praying for me and my family to get through this mess. Neither of these people had ever been to a meeting of the Mayor and Council; they just came to wish me well.

Lonzisero was standing by the entrance in his best suit, combing his hair and getting ready for the big show. He could not have asked for better timing. As council president, he would assume the position of mayor if I were to step down, and at the same time, he was running for assemblyman on Christie's gubernatorial ticket. It just so happened that Christie's aunt was also a Ridgefield resident and held a big fundraiser in town the prior week for the future governor. Lonzisero seemed to relish every moment of that evening, and of all the days to come, until the day of my acquittal. He was surrounded by the press and was making all types of statements that I am sure were fed to him by the Republican state campaign team—maybe even by Christie himself.

The meeting room was at least twice the size of our space in Borough Hall. It had been set up years earlier for zoning and planning board meetings and council meetings for when we had a large turnout of residents. A divider also opened up the area to a second room which actually doubled the size of the space and was only opened once during my tenure as mayor in order to accommodate a number of school parents protesting budget cuts for our school system.

That night was one of those rare nights when the divider was opened to accommodate the mass of people descending upon the community center to see the show, with me as the star. Working my way through the room, I didn't see as many people or members of the press as I expected, although the regular meeting was still two hours away. When I got to the dais, I saw a copy of the criminal complaint that had been copied and left for me, as if I had not already seen it, along with a copy of a resolution calling for my immediate resignation to be introduced by Council President Nicholas Lonzisero. I turned around and the two Democratic members of the council, Russell Castelli and Javier Acosta, each gave me a hug and pledged to me their full support. "Are you ready?" they asked as we sat down for the work session.

Once the Republican members of the council trickled in, I struck the gavel to start the meeting. I believe that the Republicans strategized for days over how they would handle the meeting and plotted against me. As I began to read the notice of the open public meetings act, which was how I started all meetings, Lonzisero shouted out a point of order asking for a roll call to be conducted on his resolution. I called him out of order, as action legally was not to be taken at a work session, only discussion of certain issues. Well, he proceeded to throw a fit, saying he would not recognize me as the chair and the Republicans left the dais. Since the Republicans held the majority and there was no quorum to conduct work session business, we had to cancel the meeting.

As a result, we broke and reconvened one hour later to go into what is known as executive session, which is closed to the public, to discuss matters of litigation, personnel, and other issues with the town attorney. I don't remember everything we discussed in the executive session, but once we ended our discussion and moved into the open part of the meeting, the doors were opened, and the crush began. People from all over the area came through the doors in droves: friends, enemies, residents, out-of-towners, familiar faces, strange faces, friendly faces, angry faces, and the media. News reporters from all over the tri-state area descended upon Ridgefield like vultures to get the story. They were there to see what I had to say, to see me suffer, and to write about it for the next day's newspapers. To put it on television that night, tomorrow, and over the next year.

My wife and family were in the front row with Shelley from my office to lend me support. I worked my way back to the dais and saw Lonzisero glomming onto the media. When I sat down, there were microphones everywhere, and I started the meeting at the appointed time. Lonzisero again called for a point of order to read the resolution. A roll call vote was taken, and it passed 4 to 2 along party lines. I said I would not resign, was innocent, and read my prepared statement. We then moved onto the ordinary course of business, passing ordinances and resolutions, and at the end of the meeting no one from the public spoke, but there were protesters in the audience, my political enemies, holding up signs for me to resign and step down.

As I began to get up from my seat to leave the meeting, several reporters shoved microphones into my face, asking me questions. I repeated that I was innocent and would not resign. I left the building with the attorney who had met me earlier following behind. "Is that your attorney?" called out one of the reporters.

I told him that I hadn't officially hired an attorney yet, which was the truth. When we both got into the car, he was obviously disappointed in my statement, and let me know that. He had expected me to retain him that night. We both went to a diner for dessert and discussed what had happened and what was going to occur. When we left the diner, we both knew that he was not going to be my attorney. He did not think I would follow his advice as his client, and I was not comfortable with him. Nothing personal, but I would soon come to meet my attorneys for this ordeal, and my choice was one of the best decisions of my life.

Chapter 8

BIG BROTHER WANTS TO KNOW WHERE YOU ARE

Before leaving the federal courthouse on July 23, I met with a woman who was now my pretrial officer, the individual who ensured that I was complying with the terms and the conditions of my bail. I was out on $100,000 bail which meant that if I did not comply with what the magistrate had ordered under the bail order, then I would forfeit $100,000 and be put in jail until the time of my trial. So, I made sure that I did whatever the order said to do, which consisted of dropping off my passport, calling in once a week to the pretrial officer, and reporting to the office at least once a month.

I was also required to stay in the state of New Jersey and not come into contact with any children. The problem with these conditions was that I was licensed to practice law in the state of New Jersey *and* New York, and I was a soccer coach. I came into contact with minors on a regular basis.

I dreaded calling my pretrial officer. Making the phone call required a certain inner strength even though the conversations lasted for less than two minutes. It was always a struggle to come to grips with the fact that I was being restrained in my freedoms already. Calling in made me feel like a child reporting to his parents that he was being good and not doing anything wrong. It made the nightmare even more real.

The only thing worse than calling my pretrial officer was actually going to the pretrial office, which was located on the first floor of the federal courthouse. As you walked down the hall to the area where the office was, there were photos of Dr. Martin Luther King Jr. crying for freedom and other virtues of our Democracy. I always wondered where the justice was in New Jersey while I passed by the photos and entered the office to be humiliated. Every month I would enter the office and talk to the woman behind the bulletproof glass, telling her I was there to see my pretrial officer. As I would sit in the waiting area, I always wondered what crimes the other people who came and went were being accused of. Were they violent felonies, drug offenses, or crimes like those I was being accused of, political?

The pretrial officer was always somewhat pleasant. She would ask the same questions: Was I still working at the office that I indicated when I was initially arrested? Was I still living at the same address when I was initially arrested? Were there any other changes in my life? The answers were always the same: yes, yes, and no. From there she would then make some small talk and then I would leave until my next monthly visit.

The first time I had to go to the pretrial office and meet with the officer, she informed me that she would have to inspect my family's home one day during the next week. I could not figure out why this humiliation had to occur. Until July 23, 2009, I had never been accused of violating a criminal law. Nevertheless, I knew this was part of the humiliating process people accused of crimes had to go through. The officer said that she would call me when she was about ten minutes from the house, which would give me enough time to meet her from my office, since she had to meet with me and my wife in our house at the same time.

On the day that she was going to my house, I was in a meeting and missed her call by about two minutes. When I called her back to say that I was on my way to the house, I found out she had been to the house and upset my wife by demanding to know why I was not there. Instead of waiting the few minutes it would take me to get home, she ordered that I appear in the Newark office within the next few days. I would have to report to Newark twice that month. She also said that I would have to set up another date and time where she could meet with my family at the home.

When I got home, Catherine was holding our son Matthew, who was only three years old, and crying. She said the woman was nasty and arrogant and would not bend on her decision to leave before I got home, even though I was only minutes away from the house. Naturally, this was not a good period of time in our lives and Catherine may have been more emotional than normal, but the officer truly took pride in making both of us feel inadequate and subordinate.

On the day that the meeting was rescheduled, I made sure to be at the house before she even called to say she was in the area, so that there would be no misunderstanding and we could get it over with. When the pretrial officer showed up in her government vehicle, she was accompanied by another woman, probably another officer from the department. The meeting lasted a few minutes. They came into the house, looked around all of the rooms, and left.

The only other time that I recall having a problem with the officer was during one of my monthly visits. I advised her that no changes had occurred since the prior meeting. When I got to my vehicle, I received a phone call from the officer. She was absolutely irate, saying that there were other charges being brought against me that I had not informed her about and ordered me back to her office. I asked her what she was talking about and she referred to a civil complaint that was filed against me and the borough of Ridgefield.

It took me some time to realize what she was talking about. A civil suit was being leveled against me, along with the police department of the borough, for false imprisonment by an unstable and shady individual who constantly had issues with me and the town. It was a frivolous lawsuit that would be dismissed in both federal and state court years down the line. I explained it was a civil matter being handled by the town's insurance carrier that was providing the defense, but she was unrelenting and caused me much grief over a nonissue. I guess she thought I was being dishonest and misleading, since we were all criminals in her eyes. It did not matter that I was presumed innocent at that point.

This was what I had to deal with until the nightmare was over. During the trial I had to check in with her every day to let her know what was going on in court with the case.

My last image of the pretrial officer was when the jury came back in my case to return the verdict. She came upstairs from the pretrial office and sat in a seat by the witness stand just to hear the verdict firsthand. She seemed to be counting down the days until the jury would come back with a guilty verdict, and my bail would be increased, requiring me to be even more at her mercy. That was probably the routine that she had been used to every day of her life as a federal civil service employee. Watching others who were more successful than her in life before being under the thumb of the federal government must have been one of the few pleasures in her mundane job. She seemed to take pride in watching people suffer, along with their families and friends. There was to be no pleasure for her at my trial after the not guilty verdict was announced. I would return to the building a few days after the verdict to pick up my passport that was surrendered after I was arrested.

When I showed up that day, she did not come out to apologize for the harm that the federal government did to me and my family, nor to congratulate me, wish me well, or even just to see me. A secretary at the front of the office gave me my passport, had me sign a document, and watched me leave the office for the last time in my life. Good riddance to you all.

As I left that office and walked down the hall, I noticed the murals of Dr. King again and thought of a discussion that I had with my six-year-old son a few years after the acquittal. On Martin Luther King Jr. Day he was learning about the life of the civil rights leader in school and said to me, "Dr. King went to jail, Daddy."

My response was, "Sometimes people go to jail for the wrong reasons, Matthew."

Chapter 9

LAWYERED UP

After leaving the diner subsequent to the July 27 Mayor and Council meeting with the defense attorney, I knew that I had to hire a first-rate attorney to help get me out of this mess. Being innocent was not enough. I had to hire someone who would prove my innocence in court. Public opinion in New Jersey toward political officials was not just bad, it was dismal.

The United States Attorney's Office had not lost a political corruption case in over ten years, and the last one it lost was against a police officer in West New York who was accused of accepting kickbacks in a towing scheme. I knew a lot about that case because the officer was a friend of my partner's, and I saw him a few times a month. The coincidence was ironic.

I had not had any real contact with white-collar defense attorneys during my entire tenure as a lawyer. The only exposure I had to criminal justice attorneys was when I served as a judicial law clerk to Judge Russello right out of law school in the early nineties. At that time, I got to know the members of the Bergen County Prosecutor's Office very well, the public defenders and the criminal attorneys who represented their clients in Bergen County Criminal Court. That was a far cry from the white-collar federal criminal practice. In fact, the only white-collar criminal defense attorney that I knew was Henry Klingeman, my legal defense fund attorney.

Henry was rated one of the best white-collar defense attorneys in the state and had represented a number of public officials. Winning these cases was hard, and I could not find someone who had won one since the government had a winning streak of more than two hundred cases and ten years of convictions. The West New York police officer who, at the time, was the only official to beat the feds, had hired an attorney from a big law firm in New Jersey, which cost a fortune. I probably could not even afford to pay the retainer.

My plan was to interview several attorneys from a list that I had compiled. I had already interviewed one, and knew he was not the guy. My partner, Shelley Albert, knew a number of excellent attorneys in private practice who had worked for the New York County District Attorney's office, the crown jewel of all the New York City DA's offices.

Some had even been recruited from the DA to the Newark Division of the United States Attorney's Office. Shelley had a close friend from the office who was now working for high-powered white-collar criminal defense attorney Benjamin

Brafman. Brafman's office represented P-Diddy and Plaxico Burress, the former New York Football Giant.

Shelley set up a meeting with her friend at our Fort Lee office to go over the case. The attorney showed up in the morning and we went to the rear conference room to discuss the matter. Based upon what he read in the complaint, which could now be downloaded on the internet for anyone to view, I could not lose the case, but it would be a fight to the end. He told me that the Newark Division of the United States Attorney's Office rarely dismissed cases and in a high-profile case like mine, they almost always went to jury. The logic was that if the jury found me innocent, the jury would have gotten it wrong, not their office, and they would move on to other matters. To me it seemed outrageous that the government would rather put someone and their family through hell on a daily basis for almost a year and a half rather than admit they were wrong. And then to get out of it, they would rather blame a jury just to save face. If that was the way it had to be, I was in for the fight. There would be no discussion about a plea bargain, since I did nothing wrong and would admit to nothing.

Shelley's friend seemed like a great attorney and had a great personality. It seemed like he definitely had the qualifications for the job and could handle the eventual trial. Shelley thought he would be great. She said he had a similar personality to me, quiet and subdued, which would make a positive impression on the jury. She said, in the end, Brafman would end up coming into the case to help us win. Brafman was the real force behind the firm; however, the attorney who would be handling the matter was not him. I wanted to meet with the other attorneys on my list before I made a final decision.

Henry Klingeman was my attorney for the legal defense fund and a noted white-collar criminal defense attorney. His partner had represented a number of public officials over the past several years who were being prosecuted by the Chris Christie United States Attorney's Office. Jerry Krovatin was Henry's partner and known as one of the best attorneys for this type of work in the state of New Jersey. Krovatin had represented Senator Joseph Coniglio, who was charged with extortion in 2007. Coniglio was a state senator from my district who came into office the same year that I was running for reelection. We campaigned together and knew each other well. His wife was a very pleasant woman who had worked for a criminal assignment judge at the Bergen County Courthouse when I first graduated from law school. Joe was a plumber by trade, and after he was elected, secured a contract with Hackensack University Medical Center as a consultant. The specifics of his contract were unknown to me, but he argued that he was advising the hospital on plumbing issues and its various construction projects, while the government said it was a no-show job where he made over a hundred thousand dollars. Once he was connected with securing grants for the hospital, the government targeted him, indicted him, and eventually convicted him. Parts of his conviction were eventually overturned by an appellate court, but not after he served several years in federal prison in Pennsylvania.

Krovatin had also represented Dennis Oury, who was counsel to the Bergen County Democratic Organization and who was charged along with Bergen County Democratic Chairman Joseph Ferriero with honest services fraud. Oury eventually plead guilty to the crimes and turned into a government witness against Ferriero.

In meeting with Krovatin, I had mixed feelings since his partner and my defense fund attorney would probably be a witness in my case, and I did not think it would be a good idea for him to represent me while also being a witness in the same matter, so I chose not to retain him.

I met with a third attorney at the urging of my councilmate Javier Acosta. This attorney had represented the former mayor of Guttenberg when he had previously been criminally charged with Vinny Tabbachino, a Guttenberg councilman at the time, in the 1990s. It was a public corruption case where the mayor and Tabbachino were both convicted at trial and the guilty verdicts were overturned on appeal. It would have been good to know this before I ever met Vinny. The meeting took place in my Fort Lee office with Shelley present. Discussing the case with counsel and getting to know him during the interview left me with the impression that he was not a good fit.

The next attorney that I would interview was Mike Critchley. Mike's name was given to me by a number of people. My closest friend, Patrick Papalia, who was an excellent civil attorney, once told me that while he was serving as a judicial intern for United States Magistrate Maryanne Trump Barry, Donald Trump's sister, she told Patrick and the other interns that Michael was the most well-prepared attorney that she had ever met in her entire life. Patrick also told me that he believed Mike was the best in the state, and that the only other attorney who was always mentioned as his peer was Joseph Hayden, who was the partner at the law firm that had represented the West New York cop who was acquitted ten years ago. Patrick said that Hayden would charge me too much and thought Mike was better.

Mike was also recommended to my wife by a close friend of hers who was a partner at a large law firm in the state. Ironically, Catherine's friend Dan Serviss had his offices in the same building as Mike, and eventually he would be a part of the peer viewing group that would help me get my defense ready after I had hired an attorney. Dan told Catherine that if he were to ever get in trouble he would hire Mike. When the arrests were made on July 23, Dan was on vacation in California and heard the news. He contacted Catherine once his family came back to New Jersey to make the recommendation.

I contacted Mike by phone at his Roseland office and was put through to him immediately. Unlike other high-powered attorneys, who would never get on the phone with a new client on the first call, Mike's approachability impressed me. Mike seemed to already know me and told me that he already read all the criminal complaints in the case. I filled him in on all the other facts that he did not know based upon the criminal complaint. When I asked Mike what he thought, he said that it seemed too good to be true. He told me to meet him that night at his office.

Driving to the Critchley law firm in Roseland took me through Newark and right past the area where I was taken into custody. It was depressing to relive the nightmare of July 23 over and over again in my mind.

I was a little surprised when I first met Mike. He was an older gentleman who was very soft spoken. His age was most deceiving, as I eventually discovered. He had the mind of a twenty-year-old and had better courtroom skills than any attorney I had ever seen, read about, or watched on television. His partner, John Vazquez, was younger than me and had a different demeanor than Mike but as I soon found out, was as great an attorney as Mike. They were two giants in the courtroom. Their different personalities complimented each other in such a way that it was a deadly combination. Mike possessed a unique combination of street smarts and knowledge of the law, more so than anyone I had ever seen in my twenty years as a trial attorney. John was refined, methodical, and just as smart.

Mike grew up in Newark, New Jersey, and came from a large Irish family. He paid his way through college as a roofer and worked for a superior court judge. He was eventually persuaded to go to law school by the judge he was working for in Newark and graduated from Seton Hall. After he graduated from law school, Mike joined the Essex County Prosecutor's Office, worked for former governor Brendon Byrne, and eventually opened his own criminal defense firm, working out of a private home converted into an office building.

John was a former Assistant United States Attorney. He started his career after graduating from Seton Hall Law School working for Mike. To round out his career, he left to work for the United States Attorney's Office in Newark and later became the First Assistant New Jersey State Attorney General. He spent seven years working for the government before going back to Mike's office. His experience in government work gave him a unique perspective on cases, as he knew how the government operated and knew all the players. He was also highly intelligent, graduating at the top of his class in law school, and was a complete gentleman and a good person.

When I spoke with Mike, I asked him the last time he had ever been involved in a public corruption trial. He told me that the last time was the Senator Joseph Coniglio trial, which had taken place in April 2009, and that his client, who was implicated in the investigation, was not charged. In other words, Mike's involvement led the government to not even bring a case against his client who likely would have been prosecuted had another attorney been representing him. That was good enough for me, and the more I spoke with Mike and John that first day, the more I knew that they were going to be the attorneys who I would hire. They would eventually be the ones to prove me innocent at trial and get my life back on track.

Mike seemed to want my case, since it would be his greatest victory, and John would be able to make a name for himself. Looking at it from Mike's perspective, the government hadn't lost a public corruption case in more than ten years—they had two hundred straight convictions; the circumstances for my arrest were unprecedented, dozens of public officials were arrested statewide in a bust known as Bid Rig III that was being talked about across the country; and the facts of my case were outrageous, the government charged me when I had done nothing wrong. Dozens of people were calling me, asking what the government was thinking when they had charged me because even people without legal backgrounds who read the complaint thought that it was a big mistake.

Feeling confident I found the right man for the job, I hired Mike July 28, 2009. I knew out of all the decisions I had made in my life that this was a great one. Walking with Mike to the parking lot of his office, I remember feeling a sense of calm that I had not experienced since the day of the arrest. Mike had a way of bringing serenity to the chaos. I'll never forget what he said when we got to my car.

"Anthony," he said. "When you look back, you will realize hiring me was the best decision in your life."

I told him that other than deciding to marry my wife, I believed him.

"That may be a close second," he chimed in. "But I still contend hiring me is the *best* decision you ever made." We both laughed. On the way home, as I drove past the area I was taken into custody, I didn't have the same depressing feeling anymore. I knew things were going to be all right.

Over the next fifteen months I would come to know Mike's office building like I knew my own. I had to abide by his rules in preparing for a case, which were rigorous and stringent. We met at his office at least once a week to prepare for the trial since there would be no plea bargain or dismissal of the charges.

The next day at work, I told Shelley about the meeting with Mike and that I had hired Mike on the spot. She did not know Mike, John, or anyone in the office, so she called her friend from Brafman's office. He confirmed that it was a good decision. I contacted Henry Klingeman and notified him that I hired Mike Critchley. The first thing he said was good, which I took as a positive sign since white-collar criminal defense attorneys are all about ego and for one of them to say something positive about another was probably the greatest compliment in the world. It was further confirmation that I had made the right decision. I notified all but one of the attorneys I had interviewed before as I firmly believe in being courteous and personal in your business dealings. I did not need to call Eric's friend to let him know that I had hired Mike since he declined to represent me. I do remember him saying that the only attorneys who were on par with him were Joe Hayden and Mike Critchley, which again confirmed that I made the right decision.

With my legal representation in place, I was now ready to fight to the end, to get my good name back, and to clear any charges that were brought against me. I knew I had the right attorneys for the job, and with my support group of family and friends behind me I was more confident than ever that things were going to work out. At that time, however, I could not imagine all of the twists and turns that the next fifteen months of my life were going to bring, but with Mike and John guiding me through the tough times, everything was going to turn out right.

Chapter 10

THE VIDEO TAPE

T he case against me was essentially based on "the tapes." In fact, I remember when I got to Henry's office on the day that I was arrested, Henry told me, "The good news is that the case is only the tapes." The tapes were essentially the video and audio recordings that Dwek made of me whenever we met at Patsy's Restaurant.

I knew I was completely innocent of any charges being brought against me, but with regard to hearing that the case was based solely on the tapes I thought to myself, "How could the government prosecute a case like this?" The only thing they would have to present to the grand jury to indict me and then to the petit jury to try to convict me were recordings of meetings where I sat with a person who purported to be a legitimate developer that was going to do great things for Ridgefield. I was introduced to him by a person who I thought was a decent man who wanted to put the two of us together for the good of a town where he engaged in a number of charitable pursuits.

The government's case was also built, in large part, on Vinny's statements made during taped meetings and telephone conversations which were made outside of my presence. I would later learn that, before he ever introduced me to Dwek, Vinny had been laundering money for him (another FBI-funded scheme), and earned nice profits doing it. Dwek had also promised Vinny that he would be the listing real estate agent for the residential units he would supposedly build in Ridgefield. This motivated Vinny to keep his relationship with the sleazy Dwek alive, and continue to be taped for the purpose of making incriminating statements about the both of us.

Normally, statements made in that manner are considered hearsay and not admissible against a defendant pursuant to the sixth amendment of the constitution, based on the fact that they are unreliable and deny the accused of the right to confront his accusers. However, the government was charging me with conspiracy; therefore, all of these potentially incriminating taped statements would be admissible. Even though I always knew Vinny was going to testify in my favor and tell the truth at trial, the danger was that if the jury believed Vinny's taped statements to Dwek instead of his testimony at trial, I could lose the case and my life, as Mike always put it, "would never be the same."

As a defendant in the case, I was permitted to view the tapes and to obtain a copy of the evidence that was going to be presented against me at the time of trial. Before obtaining a copy of the tapes, Mike and John, along with a law clerk who was working at their office for the summer, were going to visit the office of the United States Attorney and review them.

During this time, the United States Attorney's Office sent out a number of grand jury subpoenas to the borough of Ridgefield, which were supposed to be confidential but somehow were leaked to the press. Over the course of the several years that Chris Christie was United States Attorney, political corruption cases dominated the media in northern New Jersey. These investigations were supposed to be shielded from the public until there were indictments issued in order to protect the innocent.

It always made the news whenever the United States Attorney's Office "dropped" a subpoena on a municipality or agency, but the subpoenas were very generic and never identified the target of an investigation. If someone from the municipality were to contact the press and leak the information about the subpoena, there would be no indication as to who was being investigated. In my case, however, the Republican members of the council likely were the ones to let the press know that the feds were looking to obtain documents about me. They took pleasure in all the bad things happening in my life. It turns out the subpoenas were for information related to the ghost development company B&M, where Dwek was supposedly president. Since I never discussed his plans with anyone on the council, planning board, or at town hall, no such documents existed. In fact, the only town official who I even told that I was going to a meeting with Dwek was Hugo Jimenez, the Democratic candidate for Ridgefield Borough Council in 2009, and a member of the planning board. The only thing I remember telling him was that I was on my way to a meeting with someone who was a developer and wanted to discuss the Pfister Redevelopment site.

The fact that the government was even subpoenaing the borough for this information after my arrest was ludicrous. As a lawyer, you do this kind of research and decide if there is enough proof before filing a claim. In the government's case it seemed like they would shoot first and aim later. This information should have been requested before the big show on July 23, but the feds did not do that, I suppose, because seeking the information in advance would have tipped off everyone else that they were doing a statewide sting. Why couldn't they have proceeded with the other cases, and then double checked their information about me before hauling me into jail? They wanted three mayors, and I had to be there as part of the takedown. After Mike, John, and their law clerk had the opportunity to view the tapes, we set up a meeting to discuss what they had seen.

When we got together at Mike's office, we discussed what was said at the meetings, and all of us felt even more confident about a not guilty verdict. I was told that if this were not a political corruption case, there would never have been an arrest or charges filed. Since the feds had this long unbeaten streak of victories against elected and public officials, there was a sense of hubris among the government attorneys. They felt they were invincible and could convict anyone. Not to mention the fact that the New Jersey public was disgusted with government and public officials. Combining these two facts with the attention that these cases were attracting in the media, the feds thought that everyone would plead guilty and go to jail. They thought wrong in my case, because with every story written in the paper about me, I became more determined to show the media and the public that not everyone in public life was dirty.

A second meeting was scheduled with the United States Attorney's Office and my attorneys on September 9, 2009. I had the opportunity to attend and brought my confidant Shelley Albert so she could give me her input into the situation, which was always valuable. Shelley and I met at John and Mike's office before going to the meeting. When we got to Mike's office, we had a brief meeting in the conference room that would become a part of my life for the next year and a quarter. We then gathered all of our belongings and left for our meeting in Newark. Mike traveled with John, and I drove Shelley. We met at the parking lot outside the Peter Rodino Federal Building in Newark. I had to follow John since I had no idea where we were going. I had never been to the office of the United States Attorney, and aside from being bused to the federal courthouse on July 23, 2009, I had limited experience in the building, so this was all new to me. The protocol, the procedures, and the offices were all alien to me.

As we pulled off the highway into downtown Newark, we circled our way to the federal courthouse, which was a square block that did not fit into downtown Newark. The new Prudential Center was only a few blocks from the federal building, which was where the New Jersey Devils, Nets, and Seton Hall University basketball team played their home games, and where major concerts were held.

The Prudential Center was the jewel that former Newark mayor Sharpe James planned to use to help rejuvenate the city during his tenure. He was able to accomplish this goal just before Chris Christie indicted him for honest services fraud, convicted him, and sent him off to prison.

Christie used the honest services fraud law to indict and convict a number of public officials. It basically prohibited any conduct by a public official that deprived citizens of their intangible rights to honest services and impartial government, and was ruled unconstitutionally vague by the United States Supreme Court on an appeal from the case involving Enron executive Jeffrey Skilling in 2010. Mayor James was already in jail and had served several years in the federal penitentiary in West Virginia before the law was overturned, and he was released shortly thereafter. Ironically, the justices of the Supreme Court who overturned the law were the members appointed by Republican presidents. It was now throwing a monkey wrench into many of the cases that Bush's appointee, Christie, was bringing in New Jersey.

The honest services fraud law was used to bring charges against so many officials in New Jersey during Christie's tenure as United States Attorney that most politicians came to know the statute as if it were a part of the oath we had to take as a public official. Senator Coniglio, Mayor James, Bergen County Democratic Chairman Joe Ferriero, and Dennis Oury, counsel to the Bergen County Democratic Organization, were all charged with honest services fraud. Eventually, most of their convictions were overturned, or their sentences were commuted. These convictions, along with Governor Corzine's ineptitude, helped pave the way for Christie to break the New Jersey Democratic machine and win the governor's seat in 2009.

As we passed the building where Henry Klingeman had his offices, we turned down a side street by the federal complex, down an alleyway where parking for the New Jersey Devils was located, and then pulled in behind a building next to the federal courthouse. We parked our cars and walked to the entrance of the building together. I noticed the Peter Rodino Federal Building sign on the top of the entryway. Rodino was a former congressman from Newark who spearheaded the investigation into former President Richard M. Nixon. He was a corruption buster who did good with his life and now had a building named after him, which was now occupied by people who would push the corruption law's boundaries into areas unexplored by anyone before or even after. I thought Rodino would be turning over in his grave if he knew how the office was now operating.

When we entered the building, John and Mike exchanged pleasantries with the security guards, who obviously knew them from their numerous visits to the building. The US Attorney's Office was on one of the top floors of the building. As we exited the elevator and went toward the waiting room where we would sit until we were greeted by the US Attorney assigned to my case, I noticed Christie's former office. Where his name used to be was now Frank Marra, acting United States Attorney. Marra was a lifelong federal prosecutor who became Christie's First Assistant when Christie was appointed. The two became very close during Christie's tenure. Marra would be the person who conducted the big press conference after the arrests on July 23 and was subsequently accused and investigated by the attorney general for some of the statements he made at the press conference which inferred guilt by the parties who were only being accused at that time. The investigation into Marra went nowhere, and once Christie was elected governor he was given a plum job as counsel for the New Jersey Sports and Exposition Authority, where governor Christie saw to it that he was paid a nice salary as counsel for the state agency while he could also collect his fat federal pension. Obviously, in my opinion, he was rewarded for running the operation that helped Christie become governor.

Mark McCarren was the United States Attorney who was assigned to my case, and he greeted us in the waiting area, referring to me as Mayor Suarez. We proceeded down a hallway and into a room with a view of Newark and a long table on which sat a TV and DVD player. We sat at one end of the table and at the opposite end of the table sat two FBI agents, who just watched us as we opened our respective brief cases and took out our note pads and pens and waited to watch the show. A red-headed FBI agent who had been fidgeting with the DVD player when we walked into the office seemed to be having a lot of trouble with the machine, but eventually he was able to queue it up for our viewing. There were several tapes for us to review.

We all watched intently, looking at the proofs that the feds apparently believed would be sufficient to convict me. As we viewed the tapes, one right after the other, and took copious notes during the process, the FBI agents at the end of the table watched all of us intently, hoping that somehow one of us would say something, do something, or react in a certain way that would clue them in on what we were thinking, or what we were worried about. I made sure that I did not flinch at anything during the viewing and took as few notes as possible.

After reviewing the evidence firsthand for the very first time, I was astonished that they would have even thought of bringing the case against me. The only "proof" that the feds had was what was said between Dwek and Vinny when I was no longer in the room, or when it was clear that I could not hear what they were talking about because I was engaged in a conversation on my cell phone. I was more confident than ever that I would win the case.

Upon concluding our review of the tapes, John asked the agents to leave for a moment so we could discuss what we had just viewed. After less than ten minutes, we invited them back as we packed up to leave. Just as we were about to exit, McCarren came in to say a few words to us. McCarren was younger than me by several years, about six feet tall, medium build. He asked us to all sit down as we had begun to exit the office. He told me he knew I was not a criminal lawyer and wanted to advise me of my options. He said that I could plead guilty and cooperate in helping them apprehend any other wrongdoers, or I could have a trial. In keeping with our plan, which was to keep my game face, I looked at him and thanked him for his time. I then shook his hand and left the office with the rest of my entourage.

As we worked our way out of the building we did not say one word to one another, but proceeded into the parking lot where we parted ways to our respective cars, planning to meet again in the next few days so that we could go over our strategy. I kept thinking of McCarren and his ludicrous options. I also thought about what I really wanted to say to him, which was, since I was innocent, there would be no guilty plea. Since I knew of no other crimes—and even if I did, I was no rat—I would not cooperate, so I guess we'd have to go to trial, which is just what we did.

Chapter 11

FAIRWEATHER FRIENDS

E very third Thursday of the month, the Ridgefield
Democratic Club held its monthly meeting at the
Ridgefield Community Center. The July 2009 meeting
took place while I was on vacation. In August, the club
wanted to schedule a special meeting to talk about me and what
to do about my situation.

Obviously, I was not going to resign from office, and the
majority of the Democratic Club did not want me to leave
office. Almost everyone I spoke with, friend or foe, supported
me and wanted me to remain in office. The people who were my
staunchest of supporters, and even most of the partisans, who

had read the complaint which had snippets of the transcript of the meetings I had with Vinny and Dwek could not figure out what I had done wrong.

They all said that it looked like a case built on innuendo, and the government was counting on a jury to eventually decide that I may not have said anything incriminating, but I was guilty by association. Since I was not adamant enough about rejecting the ten thousand dollars in cash, I was guilty anyway. They thought I should have racked up style points by being more vehement in refusing the money. Some said the feds likely were going to argue that the twenty-five hundred dollars Vinny gave me was a down payment on a bribe that was to be followed up with more money in the future.

To even the most impartial of residents the case seemed absurd, which is why I think there was no great public outcry for me to leave office. The other mayors involved in the sting had all made clear promises to help Dwek obtain his building approvals, and they all took cash from Dwek. In my case, not only did I reject the cash that was offered, I refused a check for ten thousand dollars and weeks later accepted a check for two thousand five hundred dollars from Vinny's business account that he insisted was his money and not Dwek's. The proofs at the trial showed that it was, in fact, Vinny's money.

The question that residents and members of the public kept asking was, why would someone who wanted to be bribed turn down ten thousand dollars cash and then a check for ten thousand dollars, yet accept a smaller check? It made absolutely no sense unless I was telling the truth. I knew that if the case had to go to the jury, they would eventually agree with me, and not the government's case of innuendo.

The meeting of the Democratic Club would take place at our usual location, the Ridgefield Community Center, which was where we had the big Mayor and Council meeting a few weeks earlier, and there would be more people in attendance for this meeting than we'd had in a long time.

On the way to the meeting I bumped into Joe Falco, a registered Democrat of the old regime that my first running mate, Jeff Trifari, and I purged from the party years earlier. Falco was clearly enjoying the circus, as he was not a supporter of mine since the time he lost his seat on the county committee.

The local elected county committee was a phenomenon unknown to those who did not follow small-town politics. In each town there are voting districts, which is where you would vote on election day. Each voting district has two members of the county committee, a man and a woman from each political party, who are up for election every two years during the summer primary election. Even though these people may have been unknown to most of the public, they actually held a lot of clout in the political community. County committee people in Ridgefield would not only vote every two years to elect a municipal chairman, they also would select the local candidates in the upcoming elections. They selected the candidates for Mayor and Council, and if you did not agree with their selection, your only option was to run in another voting column on the ballot not recognized by the official county organization. This meant a lot, since all but the most well-known candidates could run in another column not endorsed by the local or county organization and still have a chance to win the primary election. The county committee would also vote every two years on the county chairman, who decided who would receive the organization's line in the primary election.

Bergen County, where Ridgefield is located, is a large county in New Jersey and individuals always want to have the organizational line. Winning Bergen County was crucial to winning a statewide primary election and the general election in November. Joe Ferriero was such a powerful county chairman that he was able to recruit former President Bill Clinton to attend the fundraisers he threw, and he had relationships with people all over the state and the country.

Falco loved being a county committeeman, but Jeff and I did not like having him around. We did not like his old school brand of politics. We fought to have a write-in candidate win the county committee seat for Ridgefield District 5, which was Falco's, and also one of the most important districts in town if you were a Democratic candidate for local office. County committee people also were involved in elections and Falco's presence in a must-win district for Democrats did not make Jeff and me happy, so we essentially had him voted out of office and replaced by someone else who also turned out to be a lemon.

Falco, I believe, never forgave Trifari and me for having him voted out of office. Falco vowed to eventually get me out of office. In the mayoral campaign of 2007, he worked with the Republicans without changing his party affiliation to help Republican mayoral candidate Robert Avery, but that was to no avail as I defeated Avery that year. As a result, Falco was waiting for any opportunity to get me out of office. This was the perfect time for him to make a move, and this was the meeting where he would try to push me out of the mayor's seat since he and his followers couldn't get me out through an election.

Also in attendance at the meeting were the other members of the county committee, who were loyal followers of mine, along with the rank-and-file supporters who came to the meetings, and members of the borough council made their appearance to support me.

Essentially, the meeting was an open discussion regarding the feeling of the club concerning my remaining in office. The president of the club, John Quaregna, called the meeting to order and gave a brief summary of the issue. He noted that I was presumed innocent and entitled to remain in office unless proven otherwise.

John went around the room to get the opinion of the group who were in attendance. Most of the members of the club voiced their support of me and how they continued to believe in me and my innocence. Several members of the organization said that I should resign immediately. The two members of the club who said that I should pack it in were Matt Skelley and Florence Nolan, two members of the county committee who were also in the club. Their opinions gave life to the individual who wanted me out of office, and they were plotting to take over the organization.

I was disappointed by Skelley and Nolan's opinion, but it was theirs and they were entitled to it. Skelley had been on the county committee for several years and helped us every year during the November elections. He was very active with the athletic organization in town and had been a member of the board of education for one term, losing his reelection by just one vote. After he involuntarily retired from the board of education, Skelley set his sights on becoming a member of the borough council. In 2009, he interviewed with the county committee to run for the position but was not selected, and he blamed me. The county committee selected Phil Ganci and Hugo Jimenez, something that I believe really bothered Skelley since Ganci had been the candidate that beat him in the school board election by one vote.

Skelley never got over the fact that Ganci was selected. At the club meeting, he told the members that he believed in my innocence but also thought that the only way we could win the election in the fall was for me to resign and for the candidates who were up for election, Jimenez and Ganci, to denounce me and take credit for my resigning from office.

Nolan was another story. She was a single woman in her fifties who was a longtime Democrat in town. She had run for office decades earlier, only to lose with the Vic Borelli for Mayor ticket. Nolan was an attorney who worked for our municipal chairman and borough attorney Steve Pellino. She never spoke with me after I was arrested, even though prior to that we had enjoyed a very cordial relationship. She had been one of my biggest supporters in town. Now she would not talk to me or my family, not even to ask how I was doing during the darkest days of my life. She too called for me to resign that evening.

Those who wanted me to remain in office far outnumbered those who wanted me to go. Falco had expected the club to call for my resignation and for me to go along with their wishes. Instead, this was a rebuke to his and Skelley's vision of taking over the Ridgefield Democratic Organization, and they were not happy. Skelley contained his anger, but Falco did not. In fact, one of the club members who had supported me, Jerry Plancher took issue with Falco and was then menaced and physically intimidated by Falco, who acted as if he were going to assault the frail and elderly Plancher. As a result, a melee ensued, and the police were called to the scene. Before the arrival of Ridgefield's finest, another member of the club and county committee member, Marlene Caride, who was one of my staunchest allies, encouraged me to leave with her.

We made it to her car in the front parking lot without incident, and she took me home.

As we exited the parking lot, two police cars had pulled into the entrance, and the officers were entering the building. Had I remained in the building one minute longer, I would have had contact with the police and been required to call my pretrial officer, since I was to report any time I had any direct or indirect contact with law enforcement. Thinking how close a call it had been, I thanked Marlene for her support at the meeting and for her timing in taking me home. Marlene said everything was going to be all right and told me to just look out for my family.

Marlene was an attorney who had been a candidate for council in the past, when the party was split, and lost the election by several hundred votes. She was a great candidate, and I always told people that she would be the best councilperson Ridgefield ever had. She always stood by me and the party, writing a letter of endorsement for me when I was running for reelection against Bob Avery. At the time she was the town's public defender, even after the Republicans took the majority on the council, because the police and the court staff loved her. Once Avery got wind of the endorsement letter she sent out for me, the Republicans had her removed from the position of public defender. The position was low paying, but Marlene had done it because she enjoyed working in the municipal court and they liked having her there. She would be the only person from the county committee who stuck with me to the end and supported me and my family when we needed it most.

After I was acquitted, the state of New Jersey went through a legislative redistricting process as a result of the national census, putting Ridgefield in another district that needed a new assemblyperson. When the county chairman called upon me to help him find a new qualified candidate for the office, I immediately thought of Marlene, and she was eventually selected and served as the first Latina in the assembly from the thirty-sixth district of New Jersey, and now sits in the present governor's cabinet. Sometimes good people do come out on top.

Not only did I have to contend with the Falco faction in the Democratic Party, by the end of August the Republicans were trying to assemble a recall petition since I would not resign from office. Falco, who was now passing himself off as a member of the Democratic Club, was unable to convince a majority of the club to call for my resignation. Falco, as he did before, worked with the Republicans to try to force me out of office through a special recall election. The recall effort ate up much of my free time right up until the recall election, which took place on August 17, 2010, a little more than one month prior to my scheduled trial date.

I still cannot figure out the goal of the Republicans' recall effort because it was set to take place so close to the trial date. Maybe they wanted to get me out of office so that when the trial started, everyone on the jury would know that I was no longer mayor, which could prejudice my case. Or maybe they figured I would be found innocent, so they wanted to force me out of office ahead of that so I would have to run for mayor again in order to get the seat back. I was not sure what their ultimate goal was, but I did know that they were making my life miserable during the worst time of my existence.

With the majority of the club behind me and only three people in the club who were asking that I resign, the press did not have another negative story to write about me. The last thing I needed was more bad press.

Chapter 12

I'M OKAY,
YOU'RE OKAY

Despite the insanity that I had to deal with on a daily basis, Catherine and I tried to keep life normal for our children at home, and we each continued to do what we would ordinarily do every day.

One thing that was still in the back of my mind was that I still had not yet been indicted. Continuing my daily practice of meeting with Shelley in her office, behind closed doors, I would learn more and more about criminal law and federal criminal procedure. I was still holding out the possibility that the feds would come to their senses and not indict me, making this whole mess go away.

Mike and John were also holding out that possibility and would eventually set up a meeting with Mark McCarren of the United States Attorney's Office at some time in the future, after the November election, to discuss the possibility of dismissing the case against me. Until that time, they would continue to prepare for trial and meet with witnesses.

My weekdays were basically the usual practice of working on civil cases, which, thankfully, were plentiful. My private clients never deserted me, as most municipal ones had done. Saddle Brook kept my firm as counsel even though I was replaced, which was still a good situation for me since I was still able to draw income from the fees.

Mayor D'Armino of Saddle Brook thought my integrity was unparalleled. He and I became close confidants, not only because I was his counsel with respect to all issues related to the township, but we had a special bond as mayors. Lou would always tell me that what I was going through was unmatched by anything he had ever seen. Because of his trust in me and my judgment, he kept my firm employed in Saddle Brook.

The other matters that I worked on were the personal injury cases that I was already handling. The attorneys who were working on those cases with me and representing other parties were all very kind, even though some of the cases were contentious. It was nice to have the support of my peers who always had kind words of support. The other members of the legal profession who were very supportive and sympathetic to me were the superior court judges I would come across in court.

Besides going to work on a regular basis and attending Mayor and Council meetings, I made sure that I continued to go to all of the extracurricular events in town. I would not let anyone see that this miscarriage of justice was affecting me in any way or keeping me from engaging in my usual duties, or even the ceremonial ones.

During the first week of August 2009, Ridgefield recognized the National Night Out Against Crime, as it was known across the country. It was by far Ridgefield's biggest event of the summer, possibly the year. It was run by local police departments across the country, and residents would show that they supported the police in their efforts against crime. I always respected local law enforcement, as they were involved with helping people and investigating real crimes. My local cops were always very supportive of me, and many of Ridgefield's finest stuck by me throughout this time. I was grateful for their support.

The Ridgefield Night Out Against Crime was catered by Outback Steakhouse and food was provided to our residents for free, which meant that a lot of seniors would be there. There was also entertainment, and this particular year we had a professional wrestling match. My neighbor was a professional wrestler, and he volunteered to bring his crew to Ridgefield. The wrestling match meant a lot of kids would be there, and we had the makings of a record turnout for the event.

I arrived at the community center about half an hour early to help set up. When I pulled into the parking lot, the place was mobbed, and I had to park in my parent's driveway across the street. I walked to the building through the woods. As I opened the doors, a bunch of seniors who I knew and had not seen in quite some time hugged me, saying that they were praying for me and the family. While this was going on, I saw lights flashing, and as I looked up, they were there again. The press was following my every move and photographing me at every angle. One photograph of a senior hugging me as I entered the building made it to the cover of the paper the next day. By 5:00 p.m. we were ready to start serving food. As the doors opened and the crowd stampeded into the room like it was feeding time at the zoo, the press followed with their cameras flashing. My usual routine was that I would serve food to the people for a few hours and then say a few words to the crowd.

As I was finishing serving food to the residents, the police decided not to have anyone from the Mayor and Council say a word to the crowd. They were afraid of a political attack. So I went outside to the rear of the building to watch the wrestling show. After the wrestling show, the crowd began to dissipate, and I eventually left the event. It was another successful night, since it was obvious that I enjoyed the backing of my community, who were very supportive throughout the evening. The next day the paper ran a front-page story, emphasizing the fact that I was now going to events in town on a regular basis. Obviously, they never attended Ridgefield celebrations before since I always went to them all, and this was just me being the mayor of Ridgefield. Television reporters interviewed some residents who voiced their support for me and some who wanted me out of office, but the latter were the usual malcontents who would have said they wanted me out of office whether I was arrested or not.

The other activity that I thoroughly enjoyed as mayor was conducting weddings. Mayors, like judges, are permitted to perform wedding ceremonies in New Jersey, and I had been doing my fair share of weddings. I think my newfound notoriety had a positive impact on the number of people who wanted me to marry them in town. As I mentioned before, I donated my fee from the weddings to the local youth commission, which was hard hit by the Republicans' budget cuts. It was a good way for me to supplement their budget and not cost the taxpayer any additional money. I think that the couples are now excited to be married by someone who was on television and in the newspapers on a regular basis. I didn't care why they wanted me to marry them, I was just glad to be helping the youth commission and to be part of so many lives being joined together in holy matrimony.

After the Night Out Against Crime, the month of August was usually quiet in Ridgefield politics, and Catherine and I had arranged at the beginning of the year to spend another week in Long Beach Island. We rented a duplex with my college friend Gina Geehan and her family. Gina and I had been friends since our sophomore year of college. She grew up in North Bergen and came from a family that was very involved in politics. Her father was a police officer and later a commissioner for the police department. She knew what was going on with me was a travesty, and we spent the week in Long Beach Island trying to forget about my troubles in Bergen County and watching our children play together on the beach and at the house.

During my vacation down the shore, there was a scheduled Mayor and Council meeting at the end of August. The governing body had always cancelled the last meeting in August since there was no real rush to get anything done, and there was always the first meeting in September to finish what wasn't completed during the summer. When I asked that the meeting be cancelled, the Republican members of the council refused. It was obvious they wanted me to miss a meeting here and there, so they could tell people I wasn't doing my job and should not be in office any longer. I would not bow to their wishes.

On August 24, 2009, I came back to Ridgefield from my vacation and ran the meeting, after which I attended the grand opening of Boulevard Diner in North Bergen, which was owned by friends and residents of Ridgefield. Coming up for the meeting may have been a pain in the neck, but going to the grand opening was well worth the trip up. I bumped into Senator Nick Sacco from North Bergen, who reaffirmed what everyone had been telling me: that I did not do anything wrong, but that juries were cruel and it would be a tough go for me to get through the trial unscathed. He was one of the most powerful men in the state senate and would eventually help me in the recall election.

After the grand opening party, I went home to get some sleep. The next morning, I had a meeting with Business Network International, a professional networking organization that I had been involved with for about a year. To their credit, they never raised the issue of my arrest and continued to support me at the weekly meetings, referring me business and meeting with me for business lunches. After my meeting, I traveled back to the shore. When I got to the rental, everyone was on the beach. I joined them, and we had a relaxing day just sitting on the sand and swimming in the cool ocean water.

Returning to Ridgefield after vacation in late August meant two things: getting the kids ready for school and preparing my soccer roster. I had been a soccer coach since the time that Laura was able to play. In order to continue coaching her team, I had to request an amendment to the terms and conditions of my bail order. For some reason, the order prohibited my being in the company of minors. I suspected it was just another method that the feds used to demean me. I had my attorney draft a proposed new order lifting the restriction on being with minors and prohibiting me from leaving the state of New Jersey, since I had a lot of cases in New York State. This cost time and money, but eventually the order was amended and I was able to coach my daughter's team. The soccer parents and my assistant coach, John Miano, were very supportive. John is a New Yorker who moved to New Jersey after he was married. His wife is a teacher in the school system. John felt genuinely bad for what I was going through and was only too glad to fill in for me when I could not attend a practice or game due to meetings with my attorneys or court hearings.

After school had started, I continued the usual practice of taking my kids to class and going to school activities. One such activity was speaking at career day at the high school. Every year since being elected I would go to career day and discuss what it was like being mayor with the kids in the junior and senior high classes. I had, after all, been in their position in the 1980s at the same school. I genuinely liked doing it and had a great relationship with the teacher who ran the program.

That year I was somewhat apprehensive about doing it since I had been in the papers and on television regularly. The students had to know what was going on, and I was concerned that a question would come up related to the case that I could not answer. I did not want any of the kids to think that I had anything to hide, but I was directed by my attorneys not to discuss the case before the trial. To my surprise, the kids did not ask about the case or my being arrested. They only wanted to know what it was like to be mayor, what the educational requirements were, and what the salary was. I had been giving the same lecture for the past six years and was able to answer all of their questions.

During the course of the year, I also continued to attend grand openings of new businesses in town. One thing that local businesses like to do is have the mayor cut the ribbon when they open their doors. It was a way to get some free advertisement, as the local paper always ran photos of such events. In some cases, the local news would show up to actually do a story of the grand opening. With my present situation, the press would always come to a grand opening, which did not bother the owners since they were getting free press. I did not mind either because I was never asked questions about the case, and the people in town would see me on television or in the papers doing what I was expected to do, my job as mayor. My job was not being affected by what I was going through.

Chapter 13

KEEPING IT REAL

L ike most parents, Catherine and I prioritized our children. We realized how important it was during this period of time to keep life normal for them and to give them a sense of security and normalcy.

That meant taking Laura and Matthew to school in the morning before I went to work, continuing to coach Laura's soccer team, and attending all school events, such as back to school night. I always took pride in the fact that my kids attended the same schools I did when I was their age.

One of the teachers that Catherine saw over the summer made it clear to her that we should not be out in public and should be ashamed, so we were skeptical about what to expect. Our children were at an age where they really did not know what was going on, and the kids in school did not bother them about what was happening to me. Matthew was three and in pre-k and Laura was entering second grade. It turned out the teachers and assistants were very friendly with our family, so they watched out for any strange behavior that may have been exhibited during the day and would report it to us.

To our great surprise, Laura ended up being in the class of a perfect teacher who fit her personality well, and she prospered during the second grade. The teacher took a liking to her and made her feel at ease in the classroom. She would eventually become our neighbor.

During the course of the nightmare I was living, only one incident took place in Laura's school. The following year at nearly the end of the ordeal when she was in third grade, one of the girls in the classroom said to Laura, "Your daddy is going to jail." I assumed that this was the discussion that was taking place at home with the girl's parents and it spilled over into the classroom. I did not know who her parents were, but I assumed they did not support me.

Either way, it did not matter, since other children went to Laura's defense and said, "He is innocent." I thought that was great, since the parents of those children obviously believed in me.

It was a blessing that my son and daughter were so young when this happened. They did not know and could not imagine the possibility of my being sent to jail for up to twenty years, which was the penalty I faced if I was convicted.

I also was thankful that my grandparents were not around to see this travesty, which surely would have made them ill. They were longstanding, respected members of the Ridgefield community who gave much of their lives to public service and the community. My grandfather had worked for the United States Government during World War II, and both he and my grandmother had been active in all sorts of local civic organizations. My grandfather had even been a member of the board of education for a term and could always be seen Sundays in St. Matthew's Church ushering and helping out.

They would have been crushed seeing me and my family going through this, and I was thankful that they did not have to experience it. Former Republican mayor Stewart Veale, who was now serving as the deputy borough administrator, said to me at one of the Mayor and Council meetings that if my grandfather were still alive, this would have destroyed him.

Veale died in the fall of 2009, and I made sure to attend his wake and funeral services. After the services had concluded, while standing in front of St. James Church, Veale's parish, I was questioned by Channel 1 news about Veale's legacy in Ridgefield. I spoke of the great things he did during his decades in office. Then the reporter asked me about the corruption charges.

I said that I could not comment and turned away, leaving before I was able to say goodbye to the Veale family. I had graduated high school with Bill Veale, Stewart's youngest son. He was a staunch Republican when he was younger but then supported Barack Obama and the Democrats in Bergen County politics.

Bill was no longer living in town but was at the funeral for his father, and before the services I gave my condolences to him and the entire Veale family. His mother, Nancy, stared at me in disbelief that I would be at her husband's funeral mass, shook my hand, and went to sit with family around her. She was never a big fan of mine, since her husband and I had knocked heads so vocally in public, but I had always held respect for Mayor Veale and respected the office of mayor, which was something that the younger Republicans never did. They never respected the office that I held and would act like children during the meetings, protesting the fact that I was still on the governing body. They would harp on the issue of my arrest to the point of disrupting borough business, and the people in town knew this and began to hold it against them.

They say that in the toughest of times you know who your real friends are. I lived that axiom during the fall of 2009 and throughout the next year. Friends who I was always close to remained close friends of mine. Patrick Papalia was a longtime friend of mine who was with me throughout this ordeal. A week after my arrest, on a Sunday night Patrick and I went to the Yankees Red Sox game together at the new Yankee stadium. While we were at the game, I felt that everyone in the stadium knew who I was and were watching me as we went to our seats. When we sat down, I remember thinking that the people sitting next to me were FBI agents listening to everything Pat and I said, so I did not say anything during the game.

This is how you end up acting when the feds move in on you. You think that they are listening to everything you say on the phone and in public. Even though I wasn't saying or doing anything wrong, paranoia set in and made me a different person. Needless to say, the people next to me were just a son and his father at the game, and Patrick and I had a great time at the new stadium. It was a nice way to get out for the night and try to forget all the bad things that were going on around me.

Catherine and I had always been very involved in our work and raising our children. We were usually very busy on weekends doing chores or work-related activities. During the ordeal we put chores on hold and took every opportunity to do things with our family and friends. It was refreshing hanging out with our friends every weekend and having fun with them and our children instead of working or doing chores. It was a way for us to unwind and really zero in on the most important things in life.

We would go to Upper Saddle River to spend the day with Patrick and his family or my partner Ron and his family. We reacquainted ourselves with Theresa and Frank Patti, great people whose daughters were really great with Laura, who was shy but came out of her shell when she got together with the Patti sisters. We even spent a long weekend down the beach at the Patti shore house in the summer of 2010, which was a nice getaway for the summer.

I once read somewhere that when you're up, your friends know who you are, and when you're down, you know who your friends are. That couldn't have been more obvious than during this witch hunt, when people who knew Catherine and me well would either call us to see how we were, write to us and let us know they were thinking about us, or invite us over to their homes to get out for the night and forget about our troubles for a little while. We also knew who our fair-weather friends were, people who always had spoken with us in the past but were now avoiding or ignoring us when we saw them. The Reverend Martin Luther King Jr. once said that in tough times, the silence of your friends is deafening. Well, I can say that some people were causing me to lose my hearing when their calls suddenly ceased. We would never forget who those people were.

Chapter 14

PREPARING THE CASE

Mike and John had scheduled weekly meetings with me right up until the month of the trial in order to discuss the case, prepare for cross examination, and go over new developments that had come up. The way they prepared for the case and the general professionalism in the way they conducted themselves both in and out of court impressed me. They wanted to leave nothing to chance, and we worked every angle of the case as to what the government would say I did wrong by evaluating what the law was and what was done under the circumstances of the present case.

My weekly routine was to leave my office on Thursday afternoons around 3 p.m. and travel to their Roseland office, where we would go over the case and other important issues until about 5 or 6 p.m. Afterward, I would travel back to Ridgefield and meet Catherine and the kids for dinner at about 7 p.m. at my mother's house. We would get home around 8 p.m. and put the kids to bed around 9 p.m. This was later than we had wanted to have our little ones go to sleep but under the present circumstances we had no choice.

One thing that was a concern for my defense was the fact that I was meeting with a developer at a restaurant for lunch. The public perception of this was not good. The government had to prove its case beyond a reasonable doubt, and in my case, details were seriously against them. But the problem was going to be when the case was presented by the United States of America against Mayor Anthony Suarez, and the prosecutors would paint a picture that I was meeting out of my normal offices in town hall at a hideaway with two questionable characters. They would play on the public perception of elected officials in New Jersey and use the unspoken words and actions as a backdrop of this alleged wrongdoing.

I would need to have an answer for any question, no matter how mundane, that the government would ask me. There was no question that I was going to testify and tell my side of the story. Most defendants don't testify, relying instead on cross examining the government's case and poking holes into the evidence. In my case, I actually had a defense, and we would put it on for the jury to see. In fact, one of the prime witnesses was going to be me, and I would tell the jury exactly what had happened. We couldn't let them rely solely on the sociopathic liar Solomon Dwek's point of view. He was going to say whatever he could to get me convicted so that he could whittle down his lengthy jail sentence to a mere probationary term.

One thing that I had to do was know the tapes inside and out. I obtained copies of the tapes from a facility in Newark on the instructions of Mike and John and brought them to the office, where their associate made copies of the tapes. From the time that I obtained the copies to the time of the trial, I watched and studied the tapes of the meetings that I had with Vinny and Dwek almost every day. I was able to pick up innuendos that I did not pick up on when I was at the meetings in Patsy's. Each time I viewed the tapes, I would see something different that was going on or notice something that could be used to explain an issue that the jury might have.

One thing I noticed right off the bat was that the restaurant was small and bright with large windows on three sides, not like an out of the way diner that the government was portraying for some of the other cases involved in the sting. It was obvious that the staff of the restaurant knew who I was, since I had been there on a number of occasions, and Ridgefield was only a few blocks away from the establishment.

One of my reasons for meeting at the restaurant was due to the fact that the borough hall was not handicap accessible and Vinny was not in good physical shape. He was limping around, even walking with a cane at times. Another reason was that the municipal building was essentially dilapidated, and I didn't want to meet a person who wanted to do business with the town in a building that was falling apart. Our municipal offices were not impressive to say the least, and one of our assemblypersons had said we had the worst borough hall in the entire district, so it would not have been a good idea to showcase the building to someone who seemed to want to invest millions of dollars in the borough.

Finally, Patsy's was a perfect spot for me to meet for lunch, as my law office was only minutes away. I was a part-time mayor and had to squeeze in meetings around my normal workday that included a busy schedule as a full-time attorney, husband, and father of two little children. A lunch meeting was an easy way to accomplish several things at once. I could go to the restaurant at lunchtime, and on my way back to the office, I was able to drive through Ridgefield so that I could stop by town hall to pick up my mayor's mail or sign any documents that the clerk had waiting for me. I could also stop at my house to pick up mail or see the kids if they were home from school. Oh yeah, one last thing: the food at Patsy's was great, so it was a win-win situation for everyone.

Despite the many good reasons for meeting at a restaurant minutes away from my law office and town, the newspaper ran editorial after editorial questioning why a mayor was meeting a developer at a place like Patsy's. The editorials portrayed the place as a dump in the middle of a seedy area across the street from a place called Comet Lace. They conveniently failed to state that Comet Lace was a family owned business of Ridgefield residents who I went to school with and manufactured lace materials that were used in various items, including curtains.

As part of their preparation for the case, Mike and John took a ride out to Ridgefield and Patsy's to get to know the logistics first hand. One thing they asked was why would I go to a restaurant right outside of Ridgefield, where everyone seemed to know me, if I were trying to conduct shady business dealings. The tables were on top of one another, so you could not speak without everyone around you hearing what you were saying. And everything was open and well-lit, so customers and staff alike easily could see what you were doing at the table. It simply made no sense and was only the tip of the iceberg.

While watching the tapes, I also noticed that Dwek was completely obsessed with sending text messages. I'd always thought it was strange that we could not have a conversation for five minutes without this guy texting someone on his Blackberry. As you would speak to him, he would take out the phone and text. As he was eating, he would text. As he was talking to you, he would text. I really wanted to know what he was saying in these messages after watching the tapes and told Mike and John that if we were entitled to the information in the text messages, we should get them. I had a feeling that Dwek was doubting the validity of the case as I told him at the meetings that I do things by the book, and he was texting someone at the FBI that he was not sure of the case. That would be important to my defense. (We later learned that the FBI was receiving these text messages, and lots of them, hundreds during the course of the meetings with me, but the texts were all deleted by the time they were requested by my attorneys.)

On the day that Mike and John came out to see where Patsy's was and what it looked like firsthand, they also drove the route I took from my law office to the restaurant and realized how close the place was to my office. They also visited my house in order to get to know the neighborhood that I lived in and see what Ridgefield was like. When they visited my home, they complimented the middle-class neighborhood and sat down with Catherine and me inside the house to get to know her better. I could tell that they both liked her. She was sincere, kind, and strong despite going through this living hell with me. She never showed any real fear that I would be convicted since she not only knew I was innocent, but also that I had the best attorneys in the world. I could tell she was concerned about the future, and, God forbid, what would happen if the case went the wrong way and I was convicted. She wondered what would happen to our children. They would be raised without a father and then be ostracized by others who would always whisper that those were the children whose father went to federal prison for being a corrupt public official. How would she be able to support the kids in the future? She was not working, and we weren't independently wealthy. We thought about what would happen after I got out of jail. My law license would surely be revoked, so I would not be able to practice law, the only job that I had experienced for the past sixteen years and that I had trained for my whole life. I would also be locked out of a number of positions. Maybe she would have to start working and I would have to raise the kids. She had not practiced law for years, and actually hated it, but maybe she could pick up all the cases I had worked on since I had a personal relationship with the clients and could talk to them and explain the situation, and maybe they would stick with me through her.

All of these scenarios were running through our heads, but she never cracked under the pressure and kept moving forward. She kept repeating the words of the crazy fish from Nemo, "Keep swimming," and that is what we did. Mike and John were also sizing her up at this time as a witness in the case. They had not yet decided who would be called as witnesses, besides me, and they were looking at all the possibilities. She knew enough about the facts of the case to qualify as a fact witness, and obviously she knew me well enough to be considered a character witness. Hopefully, we never would have to make such a decision. We were all still holding out hope that I would never be indicted, that once the election came and went in November, Mike and John could approach the United States Attorney and give him the full background on the case with the proofs, and they wouldn't indict me. For goodness sake, Vinny was telling everyone he was going to take a lie-detector test to prove my innocence. We all honestly believed that the case would be dismissed by the feds. We would come to see by the end of the year that this was just a pipe dream.

After visiting my home, Mike and John inspected the borough hall and realized what I and many others had known for years, that the building was a disaster. It was crumbling from the outside. The façade was falling off the building, and on the inside you could see the building was not sound. We walked to the second floor because there was no elevator. My office was in the back corner of the building. They were taken aback by how small it actually was and how there was no real privacy unless you kept the door closed. Even then, people would have lunch right outside the door since there was a meeting room adjoining the closet-sized office. Meetings would take place right outside the mayor's office at a large table where you could hear everything being said on both sides of the door.

We left borough hall and went to the next stop on the Ridgefield reality tour, the redevelopment area. We first went to the Pfister Chemical Company site, which was one of three properties in the redevelopment area. This was one of the sites that Dwek and Vinny were discussing at the meetings that Dwek seemed very interested in developing.

The background of the Pfister Chemical site was that it once had been a productive company and created a lot of jobs for residents of the town. One rumor was that the company had manufactured Agent Orange during the Vietnam War. During my years on the high school football team we practiced on a field adjoining the Pfister property, and in the summer months you could smell the pollution coming from the building and see a yellow coating on the grass during the mornings we had double practice sessions. Some of my teammates were now blaming their hair loss on the pollution from Pfister, even though genetics suggested otherwise.

Today, Pfister is a symbol of Ridgefield's past industrial and manufacturing glory. It was also the subject of a state mandated cleanup as the ground was so contaminated that it had to be remediated before anyone could take ownership. The lot was also unsightly, as the old chemical company building had been demolished, leaving a large unkempt hole in the middle of it that became overgrown with weeds. As you pulled up to the site's main access route from Route 46, there was a steep incline from the highway that would have to be modified significantly for a redevelopment project. There were abandoned truck tires all along the road. The owners were neglecting the site, and opportunists would just dump garbage there. The situation looked hopeless.

This was the area that I was trying to get developed for the past ten years, and no one was interested once they realized the cost and time it would take just to make it a viable plot. Someone had to have a lot of patience and money. Dwek's promise of being able to buy the property, clean it up, and build on it was appealing as it would have brought my town hundreds of thousands of dollars, maybe even millions, in tax revenue. My residents would no longer be subjected to astronomical increases in their taxes. It was too good to be true.

We then toured the other areas that were in the redevelopment area, Lowe Paper and what was known as the J.C. Penny lot. Lowe Paper was another dinosaur in Ridgefield, an empty lot that had once been a hundred-year-old paper mill that brought many manufacturing jobs to the area. I was told by the Lowe owners that the Chinese recycled paper at a much cheaper cost, even with shipping factored in, and the plant was no longer profitable. For a while, the building was a safety hazard. The fire alarm would go off even after the business was closed down. The responding firemen would inevitably get injured in the dilapidated building. Eventually, the building was demolished and the lot was soon overtaken by weeds. Nearby residents complained that the owners of the property were absentee landowners, and vermin were running rampant along the open space. We were constantly sending our property maintenance officer to the site to investigate the complaints and then had to force the owners to either fix the site or to pay fines.

The last redevelopment property, J.C. Penny, was owned by Burt Ross. It was the only functioning business in the redevelopment area. It was a facility that received books and other items that were packaged on the site and shipped out to various retailers. Burt Ross had been mayor of Fort Lee in the early 1980s and appeared regularly at the Mayor and Council meetings in 2004 to voice his opposition to the initial redevelopment proposal. The borough intended to take the properties by eminent domain for fair market value and give them to a developer to build what we wanted on the site. Burt wanted the town to use the open market to determine the price of the property and to buy it from the landowners, he being one of them. Eventually I went along with this idea, which is why I would meet with various developers and owners of the properties, to see if there were going to be any private deals between the groups. Ross was also interesting in another way. While he was mayor, some crime bosses offered him a bribe. He reported the offer to the authorities and eventually went to work for the feds. He recorded the conversation with the mobsters, who were convicted. Ross went into protective custody for a period of time. I always respected Ross for that and wondered one day if I would ever have the opportunity to do the same thing.

Mike and John took a number of photographs of the area before we all went our separate ways. That was the way to prepare for a case, not like many attorneys who put in as little effort as possible, hoping the case would settle in the end. Besides being highly intelligent, my attorneys prepared for a case better than anyone I ever met, bolstering my confidence that things would all work out in the end.

Chapter 15

CAMPAIGN 2009

T he end of the summer of 2009 was fast approaching, and the Republicans were getting more and more frustrated with my remaining in office. The news continued to be filled with the fallout of the arrests made on July 23, and the mayors of Secaucus and Hoboken had both resigned from their respective offices.

In Secaucus, Mayor Dennis Elwell was up for reelection, and he was facing a significant challenge prior to his arrest from an independent candidate who now had the corruption card to throw into the race. Elwell could not take the pressure and decided to resign shortly after he was arrested. He said that he needed time to focus on his defense.

Pete Cammarano was the upstart mayor of Hoboken. He was an attorney and worked at one of the best election law firms in the state of New Jersey before becoming mayor. Cammarano's job in Hoboken was full time; he had to leave his job as an attorney to work in city hall. He was also one of the youngest mayors in the city's history, and he was married with a young daughter. When he was sworn into office, Senator Menendez and Governor Corzine attended the event. Since Hoboken had their municipal elections in May, Cammarano had had been in office only three weeks before being arrested. He vowed to stay in office and would not resign. He held a press conference at city hall saying that he was going to continue to work as mayor and that he could do so even with the corruption charges hanging over his head.

Things did not look good for Cammarano. It turned out that he met Dwek at a diner in Hoboken and took money from Dwek in return for the promise of supporting his projects. Cammarano also said things that were patently offensive on the tapes. He told Dwek how he would make powder out of his political enemies, and how he would be elected even if he were indicted.

Ultimately, these words would come back to haunt the mayor of Hoboken. Almost immediately there was an outcry at city hall as many in Cammarano's administration did not want to work for him. Resignations began to roll in. Demonstrations took place in front of his home and at city hall regularly. Eventually, Cammarano stepped down, leaving me as the only mayor left in the Bid Rig III sting to remain in office. I began to feel the pressure.

Locally, however, there still was no large community outcry for me to leave office. The only group of people who hounded me to leave were the Republicans, and there were not many of them; however, they were a motivated group and they hated me with a passion. Taking a page from the Hoboken playbook, the local Republicans decided to put together a rally and protest in front of my home. They were not very secretive in their plan, as friends of mine began to call me well in advance to warn me of the protest. On the night that the protest was going to occur, my supporters were ready. I took Catherine and the kids to my parents' home and warned my neighbors as to what was going to occur. Since the neighbors understood very little English, I don't know if they understood my attempts to tell them what was about to happen.

The Republican demonstrators assembled at the Ridgefield Community Center and began to walk up Slocum Avenue, which is the street that runs up to Oak Street where I lived. As they came up the hill, you could hear the angry crowd yelling and carrying signs in protest of my remaining in office. In front of my house, a large group of my supporters was assembling. People came with their lawn chairs, bullhorns, and signs to show support for me to remain in office. The press also showed up to film what was going on. News 4, Channel 9, Korean television, and the newspapers were all there. The Ridgefield Police Department showed up to ensure the safety of my home and to maintain crowd control. It was quite an August summer night in Ridgefield.

When the protesters got to Oak Street and proceeded to picket in front of my house, I noticed something unusual. I did not recognize most people in the group. Besides the Republican councilmen who were there, along with Avery, there were a lot of children dressed up in costumes with masks so you could not tell who they were. There were also a lot of out-of-towners. In fact, most of the people who were protesting against me were not from Ridgefield.

The demonstration lasted for less than an hour, and I spoke with the press, explaining to them my position: I was innocent and I could remain in office and do my job even with the corruption charges hanging over my head. Councilman Acosta told the press how disgusting it was that the Republicans were dragging kids from out of town to protest in front of my house and how the local Republicans had to get people from out of town to protest, since the locals knew that I was innocent and wanted me to remain in office.

The protest would eventually backfire on the Republicans because Ridgefield is not like Hoboken. We are a small town and everyone knows one another in some way. My constituents could not believe that the Republicans would protest against me at my family's home on Oak Street. There was a belief that if there was going to be a protest, it should have been done at borough hall, and not at my home where I had little children and a wife.

The protest was the last major event that had occurred over the summer and Labor Day weekend was coming upon us.

For Labor Day, we decided to spend the long weekend down the Jersey shore at Catherine's brother's place in Sea Girt, which was a nice getaway after such a hectic month. Catherine was able to spend time with Rich and his family, and we were all able to hang around his pool and the beach since his shore house was only several blocks from the Atlantic Ocean. We drank cool drinks during the day and spent time with our nephew, Sean, who had just graduated from college, and traveled the world before entering the workforce in New York City as a consultant. At night, Sean and I went to a local bar by the beach to have a few drinks and just talk about life in general. He reminded me of myself when I was younger, only with a lot more money. I always enjoyed my time with Sean, and I believe he had a mutual respect for me, as we would talk for hours on end about a variety of things.

When I was arrested, Sean and his father, Rich, were two of the first people from my extended family to call me and say this was all nonsense. Sean, who may have even had an inclination to get into politics at one time, swore that he would never get involved in public life after seeing what had happened to me. It was a shame, since we need intelligent young people to seek public office in the future, and if people like Sean are disillusioned, who will run our country? Sean even showed up during my trial the following year to lend me and his Aunt Catherine support while we were going through the worst part of the process. But at that moment we were enjoying a great weekend in the sun, relaxing with our family.

Monday came and went, and the summer of 2009 was officially over. Our kids started school. Laura began second grade at Bergen Boulevard School and Matthew was in preschool at Shaler Academy. Both schools were great places for our children to learn and grow up. Laura had been at Bergen Boulevard School for one year already. She now had one of the most caring teachers we would come to meet in Ridgefield. Matthew had been at Shaler Academy for over a year now as well.

In the legal profession, lawyers usually became very busy after Labor Day weekend since all of the judges who had been on vacation during the summer and for the month of August were now back and ready to move their calendars. This meant that trials would be scheduled, and lawyers had to get ready while keeping other business in the office moving.

Besides getting busier at work in the fall, I also had to get my coaching hat on and prepare for the soccer season. I had been coaching Laura's team for several years now and was in charge of picking the members of the team and running the practices. The team was essentially the same set of kids I had been picking for the past several years, since all the kids got along great. My assistant coach, John Miano, would be helping me once again. John was a great guy, and we shared an obsession with the television show *Seinfeld*. We would often text each other *Seinfeld* quotes during the course of the day and crack each other up. John and his wife, Maddie, would help during these times by watching our children if we had to be somewhere involving the case. During the trial, Maddie, who was a teacher in the school system, helped by bringing Laura or Matthew to my mom's house or by having them stay over at her house until my mother was able to pick them up for dinner. It was people like John and Maddie that helped Catherine and me get through the tough times, and we were ever grateful for their support.

In politics, the end of the summer meant the official start of the campaign season, even though things started much earlier in Ridgefield. In our community, the election centered on the campaign for local municipal office, and our candidates were Hugo Jimenez and Phil Ganci. Hugo and Phil were both good candidates, and while this was a first-time run for Hugo, Phil had run and lost before and was now a member of the school board.

Hugo had no negatives, so his campaign for public office would be based upon the platform that the local Democratic party was running on: consolidation of services, generation of tax revenue through smart growth development, and working with our school system to better the lives of our children. The town had a variety of joint agreements in the past with the school system that were already improving the lives of our children. We shared a large synthetic field that was funded by both the town and the school district; we also financed Shaler Academy's construction, and the school would pay us back.

Decisions that were being made by the leaders of the school system were vested in the elected board of education, and Phil Ganci was one of those people. As a member of the school board, Phil had amassed a record that was constantly under attack by his enemies. He was a personable man, but he had his detractors, like everyone. His enemies were like mine; they were vocal and did not go away. One of those detractors was Matt Skelley, a Democratic Club member who wanted to run in 2009 but was not selected, so he chose not to help Hugo or Phil in their election, and in fact was part of the problem going into the election season. When the party is not unified, it makes things that much more difficult to win in a town where most elections are very close.

The fall went by quickly. We knew the Democrats needed only one seat to gain the majority of borough government, and the Republicans would use that to their advantage. The campaign was dominated by campaign flyer after campaign flyer with photographs of me in handcuffs coming out of the federal building in Newark on the day of the arrest.

The Republicans would repeat the same statement, that if one of our candidates were to win the election, then I would be the tie breaker on the governing body. The corruption theme was in every one of their flyers. The Republicans would not say what they had done for the town, or what they were going to do, but they would constantly attack me. My arrest *was* the campaign for the Republicans; they had nothing else to run on. In fact, at their campaign rallies in town, Avery would walk around with handcuffs and hold them up in the air like it was a great symbol for their campaign.

The Democrats, on the other hand, ran a campaign based upon issues and ideas. We set forth our plan to make the town a better place to live in, and we pointed out what the Republicans had done over the past few years. They were in the majority, which was not good for the town.

The election year was also overshadowed by the gubernatorial race between Chris Christie and Jon Corzine. Christie's commercials were focused on corruption, and he would say that Corzine's friends were all arrested on July 23, making me a part of the campaign against Corzine. I always believed that this was Christie's plan, from the time he brought Dwek into the Bid Rig III operation, which was wrapped up by his successor.

In order to one-up Christie, Corzine had been trying to force me to resign from office after most of the other elected officials had left their positions. I would not go. He was getting more and more frustrated. He had frozen development approvals in Ridgefield until the state had the chance to review them; he had sent the state comptroller to investigate the procurement processes in Ridgefield, which backfired for the Republicans since any wrongdoing would have been under their watch; and he was now threatening to take over the borough in some crazy way.

When asked why it was so important for me to resign, he said that I was in charge of certain functions, like the police department, and that the cloud of corruption was improper. Obviously, Corzine never held local office, because if he had, he would have known that the police chief was the person who ran the department and I had absolutely no control in this regard. Moreover, since the town was a borough form of government, I could not hire anyone without the council's consent. I did not even set the budget for the department. Corzine was dead wrong on the law and the facts. The longer I remained in office, the more foolish Corzine looked because he was giving the issue life every day that went by. Christie even said in a great sound bite during the campaign that Corzine can't run the state properly, so why should he now try to take over one of the municipalities.

When the results came in on election day 2009, the local Democratic candidates barely lost. It was a close election. In fact, Hugo lost by only about thirty votes. But that was not the case on the other levels. Christie crushed Corzine, and all the county Democratic candidates in Bergen lost by a landslide. The county executive, sheriff, and freeholders all went to the Republican candidates, and they would now be in control of county government for the first time in years.

The results of the local election were encouraging. In the worst of times, we barely lost the council race, so to come so close when even one of our own, Skelley, was out there working against the group was encouraging. There was some good news in the bad news that we had received. Unfortunately, that also meant being the mayor of a town where the only authority I had was to perform weddings, appoint some members of the planning board, and break council tie votes when needed.

While our organization was fractured, the Republicans were even more unified in their hatred of me and would stop at no cost to get me out of office before my term expired. They began to crank up their efforts and their focus on removing me from the mayor's seat as soon as possible.

With the defeat of Corzine, I began to think back to the conversation that Mike Critchley had with Corzine's chief counsel during the summer, when I was being encouraged to resign. Mike said not only should I not resign, but he predicted I would be in office longer than Corzine. In the end, Mike was right.

Chapter 16

LAST HOPE

With the end of campaign season, many New Jersey elected officials looked forward to the annual New Jersey State League of Municipalities Conference in Atlantic City. This was an event that took place every year in November, usually a week or two after election season. The weeklong conference was a way to learn about issues, schmooze, and have time to network away from the office.

I always learned a lot at the League and made sure to attend the classes and speak with others who had similar problems to find out how they had resolved issues in their communities. There were also cocktail parties and other nighttime events where attendees would be wined and dined by different professional groups and vendors. I was never big on this aspect of the League but would partake in these events with my fellow councilpersons, as it gave us a chance to unwind and enjoy some personal time with one another that we were not able to engage in during the course of the year.

As usual, the Republicans were all going to the League and had signed up for their hotel rooms at the luxurious Borgata Spa and Casino. No one in our party felt very festive with the election loss and with corruption charges hanging over my head. For the first time in my entire career as an elected official, I chose not to go. It did not feel right. I had other things on my mind, so I wanted to stick close to home. I was also waiting for the meeting that Mike and John had scheduled with the United States Attorney's Office.

When I had first retained Mike, he asked me for a $100,000 retainer for his services. I was stunned by the amount of money it was going to cost me to hire him, but I knew that I needed the best and had to pay the price. Thankfully, Catherine and I had been good at saving money. She had a great job and flourished in her position before she pursued a more noble pursuit, being a mother. I was doing well with my law practice and had a number of very good years, so we had the money saved to hire this pricey but gifted attorney. Yes, the money was for our children's college fund, but we came to realize when facing the feds, you not only had to be innocent and have the facts on your side, you also had to hire the best attorney that money could buy, and that was Mike Critchley by a landslide.

When I first hired Mike and was told the fee, Mike said it would be worth paying the money now to get the charges dismissed rather than to hire someone else and have to go the distance with a trial. At the time, I had only been arrested and not indicted. The fact of the matter was that the feds could still choose to not pursue the case against me. After an indictment, there would be no turning back; a trial would be a foregone conclusion, so the goal was to have Mike show the proofs we had and to see if the feds would wise up and dismiss the charges against me. The game plan was to give the United States Attorney's Office enough information to seriously consider dismissing the case before the indictment, but not our whole defense. There was still the possibility that they would pursue the case no matter what we presented.

I was fascinated by the federal criminal law process, since I had never practiced in the field, and was learning something new every day. Had the circumstances not been so grave, I may have actually enjoyed what was going on, but as Mike once said, I had a lot of skin in the game. In civil cases, you would by law have to disclose your whole case before the trial date, and in criminal law, you did not have to disclose anything. You just let the government present its case and if it did not meet the burden of proof, beyond a reasonable doubt, you were not guilty. Not disclosing all of our defense was calculated to protect me in case we had to go to trial, but we did plan to provide most of what we were going to rely upon at the time of trial.

Mike and John were going to give to Assistant United States Attorney Mark McCarren three key pieces of evidence that the feds never knew existed. One was the check that Vinny gave to me when we left the parking lot at Patsy's at the second meeting. The check was made payable to me, it was for ten thousand dollars, and it was from Vinny's business account. I had given the check to my attorney Henry Klingeman. Wisely, Henry had kept the check and had written the word void across the front of it. I did not know what happened to the check after I gave it to Henry, and was glad he had been so smart as to keep it in his possession in case something happened. Even the government did not know what happened to this check from Vinny, and it would fill a major gap in the case.

The other major pieces of evidence were two emails that I sent to Henry during the time that I was meeting with Dwek and Vinny. After the last meeting at Patsy's, I emailed Henry's law firm and said, "This confirms our conversation where I will not be taking the check for ten thousand dollars from Vinny. You can destroy the check." The second email I sent to Henry a few days later confirmed that I was not taking the money from Vinny. Looking back, I probably sent the second email because Henry was in Israel and did not have any contact with the United States. Instead of merely leaving a voicemail on his work or cell phone, which could easily be deleted, I probably wanted to document the meetings in writing. It was a smart decision to document the fact that Henry and I had those meetings, and that I was not taking the money. Before handing over the two emails, which told a missing part of the story, to McCarren, who had never seen them before, we redacted the recipient.

We did not want to expose Henry to FBI intimidation prior to the trial. The FBI had been interrogating all of the donors of my legal defense fund, including the CPA who was the trustee, but the donors kept telling the agents that they were making a mistake, that I was an honest public servant, and that they should just leave me and my family alone because they were ruining my life. I'm sure it was frustrating for the FBI.

Even though Mike and John did not give McCarren Henry's name, they did tell him I had hired a former Assistant United States Attorney who specialized in political corruption and white-collar crime cases. My attorneys said that he would testify at the trial if the case went that far and would confirm everything I had been saying. Specifically, that I went to the meetings, reported everything to him, and followed the advice of counsel. McCarren was told that I had given the check to the former Assistant United States Attorney, who was in possession of it at the time of my arrest and who confirmed that I was not taking the money via two emails.

The United States Attorney's Office was not getting desperate; the case was not unfolding in their favor, but they were still confident that they could win the trial. By the time that this post-election meeting took place between the United States Attorney's Office and my lawyers, many of the defendants in the sting had already plead guilty or were now cooperating with the feds against the others charged in the sting.

None of the cases had gone to trial, and the first one on deck was the case against the deputy mayor of Jersey City, Leona Beldini. Dwek had not yet been put on the stand to testify for the government. They were not sure how he would do in helping them prove their case, but they were confident that the tapes would speak for themselves. The plan was that Dwek would narrate the story, and the feds would obtain conviction after conviction of those who were the holdouts and not entering into plea bargains.

Maybe it was because they had won two hundred straight convictions against public figures, maybe it was because they had made a big circus out of the arrests on July 23 and it was too late to turn back, or maybe it was just plain old hubris, but when McCarren called Mike and John to let them know of the decision by the United States Attorney, it was not good for me.

McCarren said that I still took the money, and they would not dismiss the charges.

I could not believe it. Yes, I took a donation, but it was from Vinny, not Dwek. I never took anything from Dwek, and I even said that in writing to an attorney who was a former federal prosecutor. I also never made any promises to Dwek at any of the meetings, no matter how hard Dwek tried to get me to say that I would give him preferential treatment. The tapes showed that Dwek was pushing as hard as he could but that I would not budge on the issue. In fact, I told Dwek that I do things by the book and that everyone gets treated equally and fairly who comes to Ridgefield for an application. On top of that, the evidence that should have been obtained by the FBI prior to my being charged was all in my favor.

How could they overlook the importance of the emails, the voided check, and especially the fact that I had hired one of their own, Henry, to counsel me on the legality of what was going on? He was even going to testify in my favor at the time of the trial. Instead of looking at this for what it was, a miscarriage of justice, and cutting their losses, they decided to press on with the case against me. My hopes of bringing this nightmare to a conclusion by the end of 2009 went out the window with McCarren's four simple words, "He took the money."

Chapter 17

CHRISTMAS SPIRIT

W ith the news that the United States Attorney would not dismiss the charges against me, the holidays were not going to be as festive in 2009 as I would have hoped. It was an eerie feeling, just waiting for the news to hit that there was an indictment handed down against me. The Republicans in town were chomping at the bit, waiting for the other shoe to drop, for the news of the indictment, but it had been months since the arrest and nothing had happened.

Being the mayor of a small town, one of the great things about the holidays are the events with the residents. In Ridgefield, one of our biggest recreation activities was the holiday tree lighting. The event took place at Columbus Park, which was an area on the main strip in town. There were several activities scheduled before I'd speak for a few moments and then lead the countdown to the lighting of the tree.

The scene at Columbus Park was always quite a sight. Our DPW would construct small wooden models of the town hall, fire department, ambulance corps, DPW, and police department buildings, which were spread across the back of the area where the ceremony would take place. Then a variety of holiday decorations were usually spread out over the perimeter of the park that was decorated with things such as penguins, candy canes, and Christmas lights. It was really great, and the residents loved the holiday spirit that would be demonstrated that night. The ceremony was always around 7:00 p.m. on the first Wednesday of the month of December. Children from the fourth grade would sing a number of Christmas carols, followed by several numbers performed by the high school jazz band, and then Santa Claus would come down Edgewater Avenue on top of a fire truck, climb down from the truck, and come on over to where we were assembled by the tree.

The event was run by the borough of Ridgefield in conjunction with Ridgefield UNICO. Every year, several representatives from UNICO would be there, and when I spoke I would recognize the organization; after all, I was a past vice president and there would be an opportunity for the UNICO representative to say a few words. UNICO members would also be at the tree lighting, donning UNICO Christmas hats and giving out candy canes and other candies to the children and adults.

Ironically, in the past Santa Claus had been played by Vinny Tabbachino, and his wife Annette would show up, since she was an officer in the organization, and give out candy with other members of Ridgefield UNICO.

Even though I had never missed a Ridgefield tree lighting during the entire time I had served as mayor and as a councilman, in 2009 I actually contemplated not going because I did not want to see Vinny. In the end, I decided to attend. When I arrived, several members of the Council were already there, along with Ray Ramirez, the recreation director, Father Donald Sheehan of Saint Matthew's Church, some members of the borough council, and two officers from Ridgefield UNICO, Robert Celidonio and Annette.

Bob Celidonio was a longtime family friend who was also very close with Vinny and Annette. Bob told me throughout my whole ordeal that whenever he ran into Vinny around town, Vinny would tell him that he was going to tell the truth if the case had to go to trial, that I did not take any of Dwek's money, and that I never made any promises through him to Dwek. I was happy that Vinny was finally being honest.

Whenever I saw Annette after the arrest it was always an uncomfortable situation. I'd known Annette as long as I had known Vinny, and always had a favorable impression of her. She was a nice woman and was always very friendly at UNICO events. She and Vinny would help set up, work the door, and help clean after the event was over. They both truly cared about UNICO and donated a lot of time and effort to the cause. It was nice to see a couple making the charity a centerpiece of their marriage.

Annette had gone to high school with my stepfather and, like Vinny, my family had a favorable impression of her. She always went out of her way to make us feel welcome at the numerous UNICO events that we had attended throughout the years.

After Vinny and I were arrested, I think she was ashamed of what had happened to me, and I assumed that Vinny had told her it was all his fault, that I had done nothing wrong, and that he implicated me because of his own greed. Eventually, I would see and hear all of the other tapes that the government had, and they showed that Vinny and Annette socialized with Dwek in Atlantic City.

When I saw Annette at the tree lighting, the reaction was the same as when I saw her on other occasions after July 23: we smiled at one another and nodded. It was her way of trying to let me know that she was sorry for what I was going through and my way of trying to let her know that even though me and my family were going through a living hell, we did care about Vinny. It made me think back to the day that Mike, John, and I met with Vinny and his attorney, Anthony Kress.

During the summer, my attorneys and I went to Kress' law office in Hackensack. There, I saw Vinny for the first time since the day we were in handcuffs and leg irons. He apologized and told me that he was going to tell the truth. He asked about my family and then said, "How could they be doing, they probably hate me." People always thought that I would hate Vinny and told me that they were wishing death on him. I would always say that I had mixed feelings about Vinny. One part of me was upset that he had gotten me into the mess, but the other part was always grateful that he was willing to tell the authorities what really had happened.

Yes, he was greedy, and his greed got me into a situation where I was "in peril of prosecution," which is how Judge Linares described what he had done to me at Vinny's eventual sentencing. Linares threw the book at him, sending Vinny to prison for years, a sure death sentence for someone like Vinny, who was in his seventies and in extremely poor health at that time. Vinny was honorable insofar as the feds were offering him probation and a complete walk on the charges, no prison time, so long as he testified against me and helped to secure my conviction. The feds wanted to win at any cost and would do whatever they could to cement the conviction. But Vinny had a sense of fairness. He would rather die with a clear conscience knowing that he did not hurt me and my family due to his conduct than lie to avoid jail time. Prior to the meeting at Kress' office, Mike and John told me that it was only a matter of time before Vinny turned on me. After the meeting, it became clear to Mike and John that Vinny was going to do what was right and support me. Mike told me on that summer day when he met Vinny that he had never seen anything like it in his entire career. Mike was impressed with Vinny's sense of honor and fairness, believing, like me, that Vinny would never turn on me.

John still wasn't convinced, and he was preparing for the day when Vinny "went bad on us." I loved the way that John talked, and had I not been in the middle of this mess, it would actually have been entertaining to hear John use his terminology from the United States Attorney's office.

In order to get to the tree lighting, I had to leave the annual Ridgefield Senior Citizens Christmas party. We always had a great time going to the various events that the seniors held. Once we went with the seniors to New York City to see *Jersey Boys* on Broadway and had lunch on Restaurant Row. Every year at Christmas time we spent the evening as their guests at a catering hall, eating, drinking, and listening to live music, dancing the slow dances and watching the seniors cut a rug to rock, disco, and holiday songs. Members of the seniors were young at heart, and Catherine and I genuinely cared about them, and they cared about us.

The only problem with the Christmas party was that it was always scheduled the same night as the tree lighting, so Catherine would remain at the seniors' party, since it started at 5:30 p.m., while I left at about 6:30 p.m. to get to Columbus Park by 7:00 p.m., just in time to start the tree lighting ceremonies. Luckily, the seniors' event was held in Fairview, the same town as Patsy's, which was only minutes away from Ridgefield. After the lighting, I would quickly make my way back to the seniors' party in time for dinner and stay until about 11:00 p.m.

When I was announced at the tree lighting, I had been concerned about what the crowd's reception of me would be, and I was happy when the applause came on strong. It was a lot more emphatic than the support my Republican adversaries received. I welcomed the crowd and thanked those who made the event a success year in and year out. After the fourth-grade choir sang their Christmas carols, I did the countdown to the lighting of the tree. When it was over, the crowd began to work their way back to the firehouse across the street, which was opened for the public so that the members of the recreation commission could give out hot chocolate and cookies.

It was a great small-town event, and the residents really enjoyed attending and showing their support for the fourth-grade choir and the holidays. After speaking to several residents who had attended the event, I spoke briefly with Bob Celidonio, who told me that Annette informed him that Vinny was with her but did not leave his car because he did not want to ruin the night for me. Again, this was typical of the way that Vinny was, always caring for others and their feelings. It was the way I knew him, not as the greedy corrupt person that the government was portraying him to be.

I left the ceremony to get back to the seniors' Christmas party and Catherine, who had ordered my dinner and was sitting with the officers of the club who were close friends of ours. The president, Frank Quintano and his wife, Amy, are salt-of-the-earth people, who were truly affected by my arrest and what me and my family were going through. Frank had leukemia and had not been well but always made it to various important events.

I arrived just in time to swear in the new officers of the organization and to say a few words to the crowd. I was warmly welcomed and before wishing everyone a happy and healthy holiday season, I made sure to thank the crowd for their constant well wishes and prayers for me and my family. Many members of the organization had been sending me cards, letters, and prayers during these troubling times.

When I returned to the table to have dinner with Catherine and our friends, I was told by one of the club officers who, like me, was also an usher at Saint Matthew's Church, that a heated argument had broken out at a church social. I had been a minister of the Word at Saint Matthew's for years, which meant that about once a month I would read the gospel at 10:00 a.m. mass on Sundays. I was told that some of the members of the parish were trying to get my old friend Father Sheehan to have me removed as a minister because of the charges that were leveled against me by the government. To his credit, Father Sheehan refused to entertain the idea and most of the members of the congregation backed him up. As a result, I remained on the schedule to read the Gospel at mass. If I thought that this was my biggest problem coming with the holiday season, I underestimated just how bad things would get in the next week.

When we were finished with dessert, we danced to our wedding song, which I had requested the band play, and then we said our goodbyes. As Catherine and I drove home we thought about the holidays, not realizing that the other shoe was about to drop. The next chapter in the government's case against me was about to begin, and once again, I would be in the news on a daily basis.

Chapter 18

INDICTED

Ron Dario is a go-getter. I met Ron in 1994 when I began working at the firm where he worked as a full-time law clerk while finishing at Brooklyn Law School at night. I had just finished my judicial clerkship. Ron ended up settling personal injury cases and making lots of money for his clients after he passed the bar. He had been working out of the Passaic County office, which was in Clifton, and I was in the Rutherford office in Bergen County. Our paths crossed every so often. We would see each other at firm parties, and we would get together socially with our wives and other lawyers from the firm. It was a very friendly place to work, and the lawyers and spouses socialized frequently with one another. Ron ended up going out on his own, and we had the opportunity to work together again in 2003 when I joined the firm. I did not know the other attorneys, Shelley Albert or

Jay Yacker, before deciding to join the Dario firm in December 2002. I first met Jay when I went to lunch with him and Ron at the River Palm Restaurant in Edgewater, which is when they gave me the pitch to join forces with them in their Fort Lee law office. I had just been informed that I would be appointed the township attorney for Saddle Brook. The office where I worked at the time thought that public sector work was not lucrative enough for their firm structure, a larger firm with high overhead. I liked the government work, so I began looking for a smaller firm where I could service my clients personally and not have to worry about high overhead. Ron's firm was perfect; it was small enough to accept Saddle Brook as a client despite the low hourly rate, but it was big enough where I could have the staff I needed to service my clients. With my large personal injury practice, which Ron was willing to absorb, I accepted their job offer and began working as a partner on January 20, 2003.

When I first met Jay, I did not have any opinion of him one way or another. He seemed like a decent person who met Ron a few years prior while they were working as prosecutors in Jersey City. Ron and Jay had been the founders of the firm, taking it over from several attorneys who had lost their law licenses. Shelley had been partners with Jay and another attorney in Hoboken, and prior to that was an assistant district attorney in New York County. She joined up with Ron and Jay prior to my joining the firm. She was the only female attorney in the office but fit in well. Although I did not have any extensive interaction with Shelley prior to July 23, 2009, after I was arrested she became a primary means of support for both Catherine and me.

The only other attorney in the office was Brian Eyerman. I hired him after he graduated from law school. I knew Brian's family for years from Ridgefield. In fact, his father, Dr. Edmund Eyerman, and my father attended Saint Matthew's School together in Ridgefield. Dr. Eyerman had been referring personal injury cases to me since I started practicing law. Brian was like a younger brother to me.

The staff in the Fort Lee office were also a very close-knit group. Most of them had been with the firm for a long time. They were distraught when I was arrested and hated watching me and my family suffer throughout the year.

The law firm did not have a founder's day party where the entire firm would go out and celebrate one night a year together. The only official firm gathering was to celebrate the holidays. We would throw a fantastic party at the River Palm Restaurant the week before Christmas. Everyone looked forward to the party, which was always a festive event. Not only would the employees of the firm be invited, some members would bring their spouses, and other attorneys and clients would also attend.

The party could sometimes get a little raunchier than a standard office party, but no one was ever offended, and we all seemed to have a great time. If anyone told any dirty jokes, it was usually Shelley, since coming from her they wouldn't be as offensive. There was a lot of drinking and eating and a grab bag at the end. Ron would usually make arrangements for a ride home so that he and Jay could drink to capacity. The celebration usually went on well after dinner and dessert were served, and most times we would hang out at the bar on the first floor rather than in the party room.

This year, however, the party was a little bit different because of all that was happening with my arrest. I tried to make the best of it and not show everyone that I was unhappy during the holidays for the first time in my life. As the party went on, people tried to encourage me by telling me it was highly unusual for so much time to lapse between an arrest and an indictment. In fact, I was told that the time limit had expired and that the government was already out of time.

Normally, Catherine would also come to the party, but this year she chose to stay home with Laura and Matthew. The party was always on a Friday night, so the kids did not have school the next day. Since it was only one week until Christmas, my children were looking forward to the big holiday and a week off from school.

I tried my best to make the most of a very somber holiday season at the party, laughing at Shelley's annual rendition of "Twas the Night Before Christmas" and Ron and Jay's jokes. I had one drink, a lot less than normal, with the usual meal, New York Sirloin. After dessert and coffee, I picked up my grab bag gift, said my goodbyes around 7:00 p.m., and headed to the parking lot. As I got into the car, I looked at my cell phone and noticed no one had called. My hopes began to pick up. Could it be that the government wasn't going to pursue its frivolous case against me?

It was a quiet drive home as I thought about things. I parked my car in front of our home, reached for my gift bag, grabbed some CDs, and began to open the door. Just as I was about to get out of the car, my phone began to ring. It was John Vazquez. My heart began to race with anticipation. "What could he be calling me about at this hour on a Friday night?" I thought.

A hundred things went through my mind as I answered the phone. John sounded different than I had ever remembered, somewhat detached and robotic, as he told me the United States Attorney's Office returned a three-count indictment against me. My heart fell, and I felt faint. I do not remember how I responded to the news.

As I hung up the phone, I noticed that the lights were on in the living room of my house. Catherine was up watching television after feeding the kids dinner and getting them ready for bed. As I crossed the street in front of the house, I thought about how I would break the news to her about the indictment. Obviously, this was not the news we were hoping for, and to get it one week before Christmas was really upsetting.

I knocked quietly on the front door, so as not to wake the children, and Catherine let me inside. She could see that something had happened and asked me how the party was. Naturally, she just assumed that there was a problem at the Christmas party. I could not hide anything from her, so I let her know what John had just told me. She was visibly upset but did not lose control. She sat down and reminded me that we were expecting this news and that we would just keep going forward. I agreed and proceeded to clean up the kitchen where the kids had made their usual mess while eating dinner.

When everything was put away, she went to bed and I lay on the couch watching television, but my mind was going in a million different directions. How could this have happened to me, a person who not only would never engage in any illegal activity, but who was so cautions in every scenario when dealing with municipal business? I knew the shadow of the federal prosecutor was always darkening the door of politicians, and that there were those who were after me. I always avoided any potential conflict of interest, and illegal activity was never condoned. Nevertheless, the feds were pressing ahead with a case built upon lie after lie and would not relent in the year to come.

I thought about the future of my family. We had to pay steep legal bills to defend this case no matter how baseless it was, because if convicted I would lose everything. I thought about my job as an attorney, a position that I worked for my whole life, studying more than my friends while in college, getting into a good law school, working hard at Fordham Law, and moving my way up from a judicial law clerk to a small firm to an associate at a large firm and now as a partner in my own law firm.

I thought about what would happen if I could not convince twelve jurors that I was innocent. What if something went awry at the trial, and I was convicted of the crimes I did not commit? I had been watching a special on television about people who were wrongly convicted and spent years in jail before being vindicated and freed. It ruined their entire lives and the lives of their families. I wondered about what would happen to Catherine and the kids. How could she raise the kids with no father for twenty years? How could she afford to raise them? How would their lives be affected at school and socially where they would be the children of the corrupt mayor who went to jail? It was a surreal image of a real possibility. What would happen to my mother, who was so proud of my accomplishments and now cried all the time and was always upset and distressed when I saw her? This was why people hated politics; it was a dirty business and most people did not want to get involved because they knew it also could be risky.

I was naïve and always thought that if you had the right intentions and goals, nothing bad would ever happen, but I was wrong. The world of politics is dangerous, and you have to focus on staying out of trouble, looking at everyone as a potential problem who would sell you out for their own interests. It was unfortunate and against the grain of how I normally thought, but I would have to look at things in this new way.

The next day, I got up and began to make breakfast for the kids. As they came to the kitchen table, I hugged each of them for a long time, a lot longer than usual, thinking of how lucky I was to have them in my life, and how it would destroy me to not see them for decades. After breakfast, I helped Matthew get into the shower and get dressed and ready for art class in Rutherford.

Both of my children had taken art classes at Toddlers in Motion in Rutherford since they could walk. They loved the place, and the instructors were great people. In fact, they felt so bad after I was arrested that they told Catherine she did not have to pay for the classes. Matthew was invited to attend for free. We paid anyway, since it did not feel right and we felt that we would be taking advantage of these nice people.

I did not know the people whose children were in the class with Matthew, but they were the usual group that I saw on Saturday mornings. They were cordial, and we all sat and watched our kids playing from a room at the front of the building. I would normally go through all my official mayoral mail while Matthew worked on his art projects.

That day, after walking Matthew into the room where he would make things out of Play-Doh that had been provided, I retreated to the front room where all the parents were sitting. As I sat down and was about to go through the mailbag that I had brought with me, I noticed something strange. No one was talking to me, and when I looked around people quickly turned their heads so as not to make eye contact with me. No friendly nods, smiles, or hellos. Just cold shoulders and strange looks. Feeling a little nervous, I left and walked to the Dunkin' Donuts around the block to get a cup of coffee before coming back to wait until the hourlong class was over.

I knew the town well. For about eight years I had been the planning board attorney under former Mayor McPherson, who gave me my first job as a public attorney. It was a great town, and there had been some really great strides made under her leadership. She was a licensed attorney working full time as the mayor. When she lost reelection due to a large tax increase intended to pay for a bad development deal, which she had supported at one time, I lost my job because the new mayor wanted to "clean house."

When I got to the corner across the street from Dunkin' Donuts, I looked to my left to see whether any cars were coming and if it was safe to cross. I then saw something from the corner of my eye, the reason for the reaction by the parents in the class this morning. I had not been getting the local paper for years. We gave up our subscription when the newspaper had been unfairly and wrongly fabricating negative information about me. There on the corner, I saw that the front cover of the newspaper was a large picture of me with the word "Indicted" on top. Good news traveled fast, and, obviously, all of the parents had either read the story or discussed it before I got Matthew to class.

I crossed the street, paranoid that everyone was looking at me, walked into the store, and ordered a medium coffee.

I then returned to the class and quietly went through my mail and drank my coffee and did what I became very good at doing during the whole mess: I blocked out everyone and everything around me and just focused on what I was doing. Former President Bill Clinton called it "compartmentalizing," and that was what I began to do. To focus on the task at hand and put the other things going on in my life in another compartment to deal with at another time. I mastered the art. So much so that everyone I knew asked me how I could maintain focus during such tough times. I would say it was easy when you know you did nothing wrong, you had nothing to worry about, and you just went about doing your business.

When the class was over I retrieved Matthew and his new painting, which would be hung on our kitchen wall, spoke briefly with the women who were running the class, who always asked how the family was doing, Catherine in particular, and left the building until next week when I would have to do it all over again. Matthew loved the class, and it was worth feeling uncomfortable for the hour that he was enjoying himself.

That night was the annual Ridgefield Fire Department Christmas Party. I was concerned about the news of the indictment being the topic of discussion at the party, but, in my effort to keep life normal for our family and, more important, to keep everyone else thinking that this ordeal was not affecting my performance of the mayor's job, I was determined to go to the party with Catherine and put on my best game face.

My parents, who were our designated babysitters, came to the house around seven, and Catherine and I left for the Fiesta Banquet Hall where our fire department held its annual Christmas party. It was always an event that I enjoyed. I liked to thank the volunteers in town for their service, for putting their lives on the line to help others, and for making Ridgefield a great place to live during the past year.

When we got to the party, we were welcomed warmly by the fire chiefs and enjoyed the evening, notwithstanding the news of the day. I was supposed to be called up to speak to the group by Gary Bonacci, a fireman who hated me and was serving as the emcee for the evening. Bonacci was now serving as our borough administrator, a position for which he had no experience.

I believe that Bonacci loved the fact that I was going through this personal hell, and purposely failed to invite me up to say a few words to the crowd. I did not mind, but when one of the fire chiefs caught wind of the slight, I was invited up to the front and wished everyone a happy holiday, thanking them for their volunteerism during the course of the past year.

The holidays were not as cheery as they had been in the past, but we tried our best to keep life normal for our children's sake. We went to Catherine's brother's house on Christmas Eve and my sister's on Christmas Day. The children opened gifts, as they had done every year, and then we went to church on Christmas Day, as usual. We all tried our best to focus on the holiday and the spirit of Christmas. We must have done a good job, because the children did not seem to sense that anything was wrong even though I got a few calls from Mike or John and had to visit their office during Christmas week to continue to prepare for the case.

As the New Year approached, Catherine and I were obviously hoping for a better year. That may not have been saying much, but the case would be resolved one way or another by the end of the year, and we could then move on with our lives. We celebrated New Year's with my parents at home, as we had been doing since we had children. No more trips to Vegas or New York on New Year's Eve. We invited my parents over for a midnight toast and some food while watching the ball drop on television. It was quiet, but we liked it that way. As we watched the New Year being rung in by the people in Times Square, I thought about 2010, and was hopeful but concerned at what the new year would bring.

Chapter 19

REORGANIZATION

I n politics, the New Year meant that most municipalities in New Jersey would be holding the annual reorganization meetings of their governing bodies. Ridgefield's form of government is what is known as a borough type municipality. Its governing body is made up of seven members of the board, six councilpersons and one mayor. Councilpersons serve three years, with two seats on the council being up for election every year. The mayor serves four years. Every fourth year the mayor is up for reelection, along with a different set of councilpersons.

In an election campaign on the local level, when an individual runs for office in a town like Ridgefield, the two council candidates form a bond during the course of the campaign that cannot be explained. I had seen it over the course of my tenure on the governing body. Two people, who may have scant knowledge of one another, all of a sudden become comrades during the course of the grueling campaign season, and, if they are elected to office, they have a bond that transcends the other members of the Mayor and Council.

As mayor, I never had a running mate that I could remember specifically bonding with, but I had good and bad relations with the various members of the board during my ten years on the governing body. The makeup of the council in 2010 was two Democrats, Javier Acosta and Russell Castelli, and four Republicans, Council President Nicholas Lonzisero, and Councilmen Angelo Severino, Warren Vincentz, and Angus Todd.

My relationship with Russ and Javier was unique. Javier had initially been elected in 2000 when Al Gore swept the presidential election. He had been loyal to Councilman Jeff Trifari, my first running mate back in 1998. When I won the mayor's seat in 2003, the council not only had to decide who would fill my seat on the council, it also had to decide who would be the next council president. As a result of the decisions made by the majority of the council, Javier and Trifari broke from the group and formed an independent ticket after losing the primary election in 2004. Losing the primary forced Trifari into early retirement at the end of the year since his seat was on the line. The next year, Javier chose to run as an independent, and, while he lost the election, he was able to pull enough votes from the Democrats to cost the election for John Quaregna, the council president, and Marlene Caride, our other candidate who would have been the first woman to serve on the Mayor and Council.

Javier did not just go away after that loss. He was everywhere in town, at barbeques, at various sports events cooking for the parents, and he was a fireman who volunteered a lot of time for the community. I respected his efforts. While initially I didn't understand Javier's political philosophy and direction on the council, I came to believe that he cared genuinely about the town. With the Democratic losses in 2006, I realized my running mates for the 2007 election year were going to be Robert Kovic and James Fucci, which created a lot of problems for me.

Kovic and Fucci were not going to support me. They had been voting with the Republicans throughout the year and had tried to mount an internal campaign to have Kovic become the mayoral candidate in 2007. I had no problem throwing them overboard for two new dedicated running mates who would work with me to get elected and focus on getting the party back together.

Javier would be one half of my new team for 2007. I then thought about who my other running mate should be. It had to be someone who cared for the community and would work at winning and bringing the party back together. Russ Castelli immediately came to mind. He was a good worker, he had helped me with my mayoral campaign in 2003, and he was another active member of the community. His wife, Donna, grew up in town, and they had a son, Matthew, who was involved in a number of sports, which meant that Russ and Donna were also involved.

On Thanksgiving eve 2006, Javier and I met at the town bonfire, which was a rally for our high school football team's Thanksgiving Day game against Bogota. We left the bonfire to meet at a diner in Palisades Park. We spoke for over an hour, and he agreed to join me in the campaign the following year. I told him that I wanted to ask Russ to be our other running mate, and he agreed that it was a good idea. The next day I called Russ, and he jumped on the idea. Part of the reason for their enthusiasm may have been the fact that they had a lot of disdain for the two incumbents in whose place they were running.

In 2007, I was the only Democrat who won election in town and faced an all Republican council for the first time in my career. The Republicans were very angry. They fully expected to have beaten me in November. The next year, with Obama's landslide victory, Javier and Russ were once again the candidates and won by a wide margin. We enjoyed a great relationship, respecting one another's opinions, listening to one another's ideas for the town, and focusing on what was good for Ridgefield. After my arrest, we became even closer, bonding with one another on issues that the Republican majority threw at me meeting in and meeting out.

Council President Nicholas Lonzisero was another story. We clashed quite often with one another. He was the one who inherited a family fortune and drove around in his new Mercedes collecting rent. I believe his interest in politics was personal advancement, and that he did not care one bit for the community. He had just come off an embarrassing loss for an assembly seat. He not only lost the election, but did not carry his hometown of Ridgefield. When he attacked me during the course of the year, I would remind him of this fact.

Angelo Severino was Lonzisero's running mate, and he was also bitter with my winning reelection since I beat his mentor, former Judge and Ridgefield Council President Robert Avery. Avery was another man who, I believe, cared only about himself, which is why the Democrats did not reappoint him as the town's judge. That's when he got into politics and won during a year when our party was split and taxes had gone through the ceiling. Severino was a contractor who was the perfect politician since his children were involved in sports and he volunteered to coach soccer, baseball, and football. He certainly made his way around the community.

Warren Vincentz and Angus Todd had just been reelected to the council by slim margins. I did not think they were good candidates, but lucky to have run in two election years when the circumstances were stacked in their favor. The first time was when John and Marlene had run against them and the Democratic party was split, and the second time my arrest was hanging over the election, which was in every single flyer they put out. The incredible part was that, despite the circumstances, they barely won when any other candidates would have won by a landslide.

It was with this cast of characters that I entered my seventh year as mayor and twelfth as a member of the governing body. The annual reorganization meeting was more than a Mayor and Council meeting, it was a celebration of sorts for the victors in the prior year's election. It was also a chance for the new majority to showcase what they looked forward to accomplishing in the new year. There would also be new appointments if a new majority had just taken control.

The fact that the Republicans had been in the majority since January 2007 meant that their professionals—attorney, auditor, engineer, and other department heads—would remain the same unless something unusual happened. When I received the agenda and scanned through the appointments the week before the meeting, it was obvious that the Republicans were going to keep their team in place. With regard to their focus in the upcoming year, they would not say exactly what they were going to do, other than try to get me out of office with every fiber in their bodies and make my family's life miserable.

Since the Republicans had no changes in their hires for 2009 and did not demonstrate any new direction for the town, all that was left for them was to celebrate their November election victory with Republicans from across the county. It was a great year to be a Republican in the state of New Jersey, as they won a number of local council races, the sheriff and executive posts in Bergen County, and, most important, Christopher Christie, the former United States Attorney appointed by former President George W. Bush, had won his race for governor, defeating a limp and lifeless Jon Corzine by a ridiculously wide margin of victory. It was embarrassing for Corzine since he sank so much more money into the campaign than Christie. Corzine had President Obama stump for him on several occasions, and even had Vice President Joe Biden visit over the summer. Despite all the money and high-profile supporters Corzine was crushed, and he took down a number of good public servants with him, like our own county executive Dennis McNerney, who was defeated as a result of the Republican landslide. New Jersey was suddenly a red state.

I had several theories as to why Corzine lost the election. He was just a bad governor. He did not do anything that helped with the property tax crisis, which is always the number one issue in New Jersey. His oratorical skills did not stand a chance against the charismatic Christie. And he upset the Democratic establishment so much that they did not help get out the vote for him.

As I've recounted, Corzine was no friend of mine. During my time of crisis, he only made things worse by pressuring me to resign. He continually did whatever he could to make me look bad in town. He issued an executive order to hurt my constituents if I did not resign, and he continually offered sound bites to the press about corrupt politicians and why I needed to leave office. It not only angered me and my family, but all the Democrats in Bergen County who knew that I was innocent, so much so that many Democrats told me they did not vote for Corzine because of what he did to me.

Corzine also angered many establishment Democrats when he called for the resignation of a member of his cabinet who was targeted on the day of the arrests. Joseph Doria, a former mayor of Bayonne and senator from Hudson County who was well liked by the people, had somehow gotten wrapped up in the sting. The cameras were rolling when the FBI carried boxes out of his home. It was later revealed that the boxes were empty. The feds hadn't found anything incriminating in his home, but since the cameras were there, they had to make a show of it. The FBI actually took empty boxes out of Doria's house to look like something was discovered. Doria was never arrested, charged, or accused of doing anything wrong. Nevertheless, Corzine rushed to judgment, like many in the public, and called for his resignation. This upset so many of Doria's supporters, who turned their backs on Corzine.

The election of 2009 brought victory to two Republican freeholders who were at the reorganization meeting to swear in Vincentz and Todd. The crowd of Republican appointees and supporters cheered them on while Javier, Russ, and I sat there watching the celebration. It was another year of being in the minority and having no input on any of the major issues of the day. It was upsetting to watch the Republicans running the town yet again.

The only difference this year was the trial hanging over my head, and I would be reminded of it with every meeting that I attended, every activity that I participated in, and every day that I lived. I could not wait for the nightmare to be over, but it was still a long way off.

Chapter 20

THE TRIAL

I was not looking forward to the next phase of the proceedings against me. My arraignment in Newark's Federal District Court was on January 20, 2010. I had to appear before the Honorable Jose Linares. Vinny would also be there. The arraignment was a formality in the process where those accused appeared before the court and were informed of the charges against them.

Catherine and Shelley came with me to show support. The trial date was set for April, but Mike and John asked for a delay so they could have time to get other evidence that the government was required to turn over. This extra time would also give the government a chance to flip Vinny against me, but they underestimated him. Vinny would not budge on any offer the government made, no matter how great a deal. I heard the feds offered Vinny probation, no jail time, in other words a complete walk, if he were to testify against me. Vinny stuck to his guns, insisting that I did nothing wrong. In the end, he was given no leniency for his crimes. In the end, he told the truth and did not hurt me, which was all that I had hoped for.

On arraignment day, Catherine, Shelley, and I traveled to the Critchley firm in Roseland and discussed what would occur. Shelley had already explained to Catherine and me what to expect. When we arrived at Critchley's office, Mike and John went into detail as to what was going to happen and what I should do throughout the hearing in court. When we arrived in Newark, we parked in the lot that Mike and John always used behind the courthouse and walked around to the front entrance where we had to navigate through the media taking pictures to get to the large front doors. Prior to my arrest on July 23, 2009, I had only good experiences in the federal courthouse, settling cases for my clients. Now, I dreaded going in. Not only did I have to run the media gamut, I had to make my appearance in the office of the always wonderful pretrial officer who was counting the days until my conviction.

Before we went up to the third-floor courtroom of the Honorable Jose Linares, I checked in with the pretrial officer and went through the usual mundane questions: "Still at the same job, address, no changes in status?" The answers were always the same, but on that day, I added that I was going to be arraigned. I always had to watch what I said to the pretrial officer, since any wrong answer would lead to a ballistic reaction and her recommending revocation of my bail and having me thrown in jail. When I finished with my pretrial appearance I joined the party upstairs in the courtroom.

Everyone was still waiting for the judge to enter. Mike and John were speaking with the United States Attorneys who would by trying the case, Mark McCarren and Maureen Nakly, probably about when the trial would start and procedures that would have to take place before the trial.

While we were waiting for the proceedings to begin, I saw Brian Neary, who was a reputable criminal defense attorney widely known in Bergen County. Brian was representing Leona Beldini, the deputy mayor of Jersey City. I specifically remember Beldini from that infamous day in July as she was the only woman brought into the circuslike courtroom when we were all informed of the charges against each and every one of us. The magistrate also told us that we could be facing twenty years in jail and hundreds of thousands of dollars in fines if we were found guilty.

Beldini's case was scheduled to go to trial in less than a month, and Brian was just receiving the government's documents, dozens of boxes of evidence pertaining to Dwek and other information related her case. Brian's associate looked shocked at the amount of documentation being turned over for review. It seemed like a massive amount of material for someone to go through at all, no less than in a month. But Brian's approach was to tell the government to bring it on: no plea bargains, no negotiations, no extensions, which also meant that he did not get extra time to prepare. In the end, Brian's strategy did not work. More on that later.

Beldini was in her late seventies. The tapes of her case were posted online by the media, and you could see that Dwek was taking advantage of an old woman, as he did everyone he came into contact with, by pushing words into their conversation. Beldini was not the true target of the investigation—the feds were hoping to get the mayor of Jersey City, Jeremiah Healey—but to her credit, Beldini never flipped on Healey, and he was never charged with anything. The Beldini case was much different than my case.

Essentially, the case centered on donations that Dwek made to the reelection campaign of Mayor Healey who was up for election in May of 2009. The feds put the master criminal Dwek in the middle of a number of Hudson County municipal campaigns. These campaigns were all taking place at the same time and were separate from almost every other election in the state of New Jersey because of the form of government for most Hudson County towns.

Christie's plan, I believe, was to take down as many elected officials and political operatives as possible before the gubernatorial election in the fall, so he could smash the Democratic machine in Hudson and win the statewide election. The only problem was that many of the individuals Dwek was dealing with were bottom feeders on the political chain who would say whatever they could to make themselves look more important than they actually were. Dwek was rarely able to get the big fish, namely a mayor, to a meeting.

In Beldini's case, the mayor of Jersey City actually showed up for a meeting, but he was never charged. Instead, they got Beldini for extortion and accepting a bribe on behalf of Mayor Healey, since she was the treasurer of the campaign. The theory was that Beldini would benefit from Healey's being reelected, so she was charged with a number of crimes.

Beldini had met with Dwek about developing a dilapidated underutilized site in Jersey City—an impoverished area screaming for a new tax base. When Beldini began to exit the restaurant,

Dwek jumped up from the table and followed her out the door, spewing incriminating statements in hopes of getting Beldini to bite. It looked like Beldini did not hear even half of the things that Dwek had been saying. Then she made some innocuous responses, probably trying to be polite to the pushy and obnoxious sociopath. She probably never would have been in a meeting with Dwek had it not been for the municipal bottom feeders who roped her in, and eventually testified against her.

The money that was involved in the Beldini case came in the form of checks from Dwek to the campaign for Healey. It was obvious to me that Christie wanted Healey, mayor of the second biggest city in New Jersey. Beldini would never testify against Healey, and she would pay the price when convicted. She was sentenced to three years in Federal Prison, what could have been a surefire death sentence for an elderly woman who was in bad health.

The second conviction for the feds was Daniel Van Pelt, an assemblyman from Ocean County, New Jersey. Van Pelt was the only Republican who was arrested in the sting operation. Ocean County was heavily dominated by Republican officeholders, and the way that Van Pelt was dragged into the sting was through a former Hudson County politician who was now living in Ocean County. When Dwek came looking for victims, he spoke with a Democratic leader in Jersey City who knew a Democratic leader in Ocean County who knew enough to put Dwek in touch with the Republican leader of Ocean County, since the Democrats were not in the majority. That official, who was never charged, put Dwek in touch with Van Pelt, a Republican assemblyman.

With that convoluted game of connect the dots, Van Pelt, a former mayor from a small beach town in Ocean County, New

Jersey, who rose to become a state assemblyman, was brought into the Bid Rig III circle. I remember Van Pelt vividly on the date of the arrests. He looked like a surfer dude with his khaki pants and boat shoes and beach look. I wondered who this guy was and how he was involved.

When we were being processed by the US Marshals Service and Van Pelt was asked about his profession, he replied that he *was* an assemblyman. I read online after the arrests that Van Pelt had resigned his office almost immediately and was terminated from his job as the borough administrator of a neighboring Ocean County town. When I read the updates on his trial in May, I found out he was convicted of all charges.

Van Pelt, unlike Beldini, did testify at his trial in United States District Court in Trenton, which was the only Bid Rig III trial that did not take place in Newark Federal District Court. His case was not as widely covered as all the cases in Newark. Van Pelt was seen on tape taking money from Dwek at Morton's restaurant in Atlantic City, in a doggie bag.

After watching the tapes of Van Pelt, I had a hard time making out just what promises he had made to Dwek. It was more and more apparent that if someone took money from Dwek, the government would make whatever case it could. It really did not matter what was discussed at the meetings. If you took money, you got charged, and either plead guilty or went to trial. Van Pelt was sentenced to more than three years in federal prison. He was the second Bid Rig III defendant in a row to be convicted at the time of trial, and the government was getting more and more comfortable with Dwek as their witness. In return for their convictions, Dwek would get favorable treatment at his eventual sentencing. The cooperation agreement with Dwek and the feds was working out in both their favors.

Mike and John were still speaking with the prosecutors when Judge Linares came into the courtroom. The courtroom deputy shouted, "All rise," and everyone stood. Catherine and Shelley were still speaking with Brian and his associate.

Judge Linares was born in Cuba, a Republican appointment nominated by President Bush. Judge Linares had also been supported by Senator Robert Menendez, a Democrat from Hudson County, which was where Judge Linares had grown up and gone to school. Mike and John were happy that Judge Linares had the case and they assured me he would conduct a fair trial.

The judge asked everyone to be seated and read out the caption of the case: "This is the case of the United States of America vs. Anthony R. Suarez." Just hearing those words was numbing. The country that my family had served in either the military or in governmental service during World War II— including time with NASA in the 1960s—was charging me with a crime. I was now defending myself against the United States in a political corruption case. It was surreal, and I could tell by the look in Catherine's face that she was just as shocked and dumbfounded as I was.

It was a short proceeding. The judge picked a trial date in October and set dates for motions, which would be over the summer. He demanded that the government provide all the tapes that had not yet been provided, along with clear copies of the ones that were already handed over, which were defective in many areas essential to the case. When we left the federal building, I was anxious to obtain the tapes, so I went to the facility in Newark where I could get copies. I then brought them right to the

Critchley law office where Mike and John would eventually comb through the hours and hours of meetings, one by one, and come up with a treasure trove of information that we would eventually use in the defense in the fall. What we soon found made the government's case against me even more egregious than we initially thought. With Mike and John at the helm of my defense, everyone who was following this travesty of justice would soon see just how bad the government wanted to get me, and how the feds would pull out all the stops to obtain a conviction once in their crosshairs.

Yes, this prosecution commenced under Chris Christie, the new governor of New Jersey, but it was now being conducted by his successors, who would stop at nothing to win the case.

Chapter 21

NO APPEAL
NECESSARY

I n 2004, the Mayor and Council of Ridgefield held a town hall meeting that was widely attended by local residents. The meeting was held at the suggestion of a political consultant I had hired that year, and came on the heels of a number of major issues for the town. One issue was the redevelopment of the Pfister site and other surrounding properties that had been gathering steam, and the other was the recent state mandated revaluation of the borough's properties.

In a revaluation, all properties in the town are reassessed and new values are attached to the properties. The process took place in 2003 and the new values hit the tax bills in 2004, my first year as mayor. As a result of the revaluation, homeowner's taxes increased by as much as 50 percent, a staggering number for a community loaded with senior citizens who were living on fixed incomes.

The redevelopment was a way to boost the tax base, thereby alleviating the burden on the current taxpayers in town. The owners of the old factories waged a public relations campaign against me and the council that turned the media against us, and we received a lot of negative press. What else was new?

The press continued to follow their motto: don't let the facts get in the way of a good story. They reported that families were going to be displaced and businesses were going to be shut down. Nothing could have been further from the truth. What we did was try to get a plan for the future of the area and look into our options to bring tax ratables to Ridgefield, something that had been given only lip service for years by past administrations. The press whipped people into such a frenzy that hundreds and hundreds of residents filled up the community center to voice their disapproval. They held up signs and shouted, "Recall."

The threat of a recall election against me and several councilmen was real. The Republicans were planning to take the extreme step of rallying residents to sign a petition and place a question on the ballot for a special election asking if the mayor and councilmen should be removed from office.

This recall ballot never came to fruition in 2004, but after I was arrested and refused to step down in 2009, Republican Municipal Chairman Robert Avery and his crew began to crank up the recall idea again.

The recall process was time-consuming. After getting the recall petition certified by the town clerk, Republicans had to go out and get 25 percent of the residents who voted in the previous election to sign it. There were strict guidelines for signing the petition. The signatories had to be residents. They had to add their address. They had to initial that they read the petition and understood what it said and then they had to sign the petition. There was a second signature line which had to be signed by the person witnessing the individual signing the petition. When a page of the petition was filled up with signatures, it had to be signed and notarized. It was all very convoluted and intended to discourage recall elections from taking place, since it was written by lawmakers who were effectively giving voters the ability to take them out of office. The recall election could also only take place after the office holder had completed the first year of his or her term, and the signatures need to be obtained in a fixed window of time.

Getting someone to sign a recall petition was pretty heady stuff for a resident, since they would be signing a public document, and everyone would know this, including me. I had learned over the course of my political career that people could tell you they loved you and would vote for you to your face, but once they got behind the curtain in the election booth, they could vote for someone else. When someone signed the recall petition, which effectively said that they wanted to remove the stain from the mayor's seat, it was obvious that the signer no longer wanted me around.

Due to the endless procedural obstacles, Steve Pellino, who ended up representing me in defense of the recall effort, was confident the Republicans would never get enough signatures for the recall. With that, we essentially sat back and watched the Republicans struggle with the first attempt. They submitted their first petition in August and found out they had only fourteen days to get the necessary signatures to make it on the November ballot.

The recall committee, which consisted of Robert Avery, Nicholas Lonzisero, and Angus Todd, failed miserably. As a result of this embarrassing episode, the Republicans were more determined than ever to succeed at the recall. They doubled down on their efforts and went on a second mission to gather the necessary signatures. By then, the committee had reconstituted itself; it was now Avery, Todd, and former Republican Councilman Thomas Blackley, all three individuals who had testified against me in the Mecca trial, and they faced another problem: borough clerk, Martin Gobbo, or Marty as we called him. When the committee submitted a second petition in October, Marty refused to certify it, saying the committee had already submitted a petition and therefore had to wait a year before submitting another petition. He rejected the document.

As a result of Marty's rejection of the petition, Avery, who was a mediocre attorney in my opinion and had no experience in election law, filed a complaint in the Superior Court of New Jersey, Bergen County, to have a judge order that the clerk certify the petition and allow the recall to proceed because he said the first petition was withdrawn and therefore didn't count. The case was assigned to Judge Robert Wilson, a jurist that I had a number of cases with in my private practice and who seemed to be a middle of the road member of the bench.

Under any other set of facts and circumstances, the borough would automatically provide an attorney for a municipal employee who was being sued. That would not happen in this case. Marty requested representation from the council and offered two attorneys to represent him, one Democrat and one Republican. The council outright denied his request. As a result, Marty went to court on his own, and the judge immediately ruled that he had to accept the petition and that the committee could immediately start collecting signatures.

Since Steve Pellino thought Marty legally was on shaky ground, the result was not completely unexpected. We now braced for the new attempt by the Republican recall committee to gather the signatures that were necessary for the recall election. Steve and the rest of the Democratic organization did not give much credence to this threat, as the workload was ominous and the fact that the petition was certified for collecting signatures just before Election Day in November 2009 meant that the Republicans would have to be going door to door through the dead of winter to gather enough signatures by the end-of-March deadline. It was unheard of for a committee to be able to gather the thousands of signatures necessary, not to mention having an election in the end.

The Republicans pushed hard for signatures on Election Day. They stood in front of the various polling places, trying to get people to sign the document. This was a smart move, since the people who were voting were obviously tuned into what was going on in town. Avery and company would be able to reach a lot of people at a neutral location instead of having to bother them at their homes on the weekend or at night. Initially, I thought the committee was not having much luck since most people did not want to sign the document or were outright hostile when being approached to sign it. I felt good about what was happening and did not think the committee would ever obtain enough signatures and would actually become discouraged by the reaction of the residents they were harassing. I was wrong in both respects.

I had heard reports from various residents that the committee and their minions were experiencing great difficulty in their trek to gather signatures. People told me stories of seeing Vincentz, the Republican candidate for mayor, trudging through the snow in the dead of winter. He was going door to door morning, noon, and evening, and on weekends, on a mission to gather enough signatures. He saw me as vulnerable and wanted to be mayor more than anything.

During a severe snowstorm in January 2010, a friend of mine told me that Todd went to his door asking if he and his wife would be willing to sign the petition. Todd did not know that the man and his wife were friendly with Catherine and me. They told him that he should be out helping the shut-ins shovel out of their homes rather than bothering people for their signatures.

No confrontation discouraged the Republicans. Even though the inner circle of Democratic leaders continued to doubt the ability of the Republicans to gather enough signatures, I was concerned. The weather had broken by the middle of March, and I would still see Todd or Severino walking down the block on a Sunday with clipboard in hand knocking on doors. "Why would they continue to gather signatures if the effort was futile?" I wondered. There had to be something going on and it wasn't good for me.

By the end of March, a hotly contested school board election was taking place in town. Phil Ganci's seat was up, and he was just coming off a defeat after running for council as a Democrat the previous November. Phil's opponents were Lisa Bicocchi, a friend of mine, and Salvatore Zisa, one of my mortal enemies in town. Zisa was one of the godfathers of the recall effort. He was sinking massive amounts of time into the recall effort. It had become a personal obsession for him and was downright scary.

Zisa was a former Republican councilman who was defeated by Javier Acosta in 2000. I had run against him and came within six votes in the only election that I had ever lost. I challenged the results. I always believed Zisa never forgave the fact that I had the audacity to challenge his victory, and from that point on, he was determined to destroy me and my legacy in town. Zisa always came off as a nice and affable older man, but I knew him as a wolf in sheep's clothing; I could see through his game.

There was a fundraiser for the Zisa-Bicocchi ticket at the community center during the last weekend in March 2010, one week before the recall petition was to be turned in to the clerk. I learned from a friend of mine who was a former Republican councilman that many Republicans who had been involved in the recall campaign were at the center and were talking about the petition. My friend had refused to sign the petition but said the Republicans and their committee had gathered hundreds more signatures than needed and were going to turn in the petition that Monday. I was shocked and immediately called Steve Pellino. He doubted they had the signatures and even if they did, assumed that most of the signatures were invalid.

Sure enough, that Monday, true to form and always looking to get his mug in the paper, Avery hand-delivered the petition to the new acting borough clerk, Linda Silvestri. (Marty Gobbo's term had expired in December and he obviously was not reappointed by the Republicans.) Linda had been the assistant borough clerk and was a Republican appointment from years ago. She had always been a straight shooter, and I had every confidence in her abilities. Linda did not like the limelight, and Avery had a newspaper photographer at town hall the morning he delivered the petition. You could see Avery grinning in the photo with Linda trying to hide her face. The headline said Avery was delivering the recall petition calling for a special election.

The next step was for Linda to certify that each name on the petition matched the voter's signature on file, and that each person was registered to vote at the location indicated on the petition. As Linda was going through the petition, Hugo and I also combed through the hundreds of pages of signatures, checking to see if they were proper. We also looked to see if there were other irregularities in the petition. What we found was quite disturbing.

There were many signatures of the same person on multiple pages, and their signatures did not even match one another. Many people were not registered at the addresses that were listed on the petition. Some pages were not notarized, and many people never initialed the areas where the signer had to indicate that he or she read the petition and understood what they had read. Hugo and I reported these results to Steve Pellino, who sent a letter to Linda demanding further review and investigation. As a result, Linda did not certify the petition, and the Republicans became more and more frustrated. They tried to correct the defects but could not correct enough to get over the threshold. Avery went to court again.

The case was still assigned to Judge Wilson, who scheduled a hearing on the petition in late May. Even if we were to lose the hearing, I figured Judge Wilson would have to set a trial date after my October corruption trial. I assumed my corruption trial would result in my vindication, and the recall election would become a moot point, but this was not to be the case.

Judge Wilson heard the case in one day and less than a week later ruled that the recall election be held in August, less than two months before the start of my corruption trial. Steve Pellino filed the requisite paperwork for an appeal, and we were convinced that the appellate court would overturn the decision. Unfortunately, the appellate division did not give our appeal as much credence as we thought and affirmed Judge Wilson's decision almost immediately. Our next step was to go to the New Jersey Supreme Court. To my recollection, the Supreme Court refused to hear the appeal, in effect affirming the Appellate Division opinion. I could not figure out how this could happen.

Whatever the court's reasons, there would now be a recall election on August 17, 2010, the first in Ridgefield's history. I was facing daunting odds, since no elected official had ever won a recall election in New Jersey and, with the federal corruption charges hanging over my head, I was not sure what the outcome would be. There I was; after winning election in 2007, I now had to run in another race less than three years later, and it would be an uphill battle. I would campaign as if this were my last election and in a way that I had never campaigned before.

Chapter 22

RECALL ELECTION

I loved to campaign for office. I can remember back to my first campaign in 1997 when the Ridgefield Democratic organization had no money, could not find a running mate for me, and no one was around to help on election day. When I made my first run for mayor in 2003, all that had changed. The campaign treasury was flush after years of winning elections and victory parties. Everyone wanted to help year-round, and there was an abundance of people who wanted to run for office.

In the summer of 2010, though, I was not up to running another campaign. I needed to focus on my upcoming corruption trial and keeping my practice afloat so that I could pay legal bills and continue to represent the borough of Ridgefield in the best way that I could under the circumstances. From the day Sergeant Jose Brito of the Ridgefield Police Department served me notice of the recall election, I was locked in campaign mode for the next three months.

I remember that day well. I was at the home of a constituent, helping her with some legal issues. Jose knew where I was that day, so he agreed to deliver the notice personally. When he showed up, he was visibly upset that he had to give me the notice. He would be one of the police officers from the borough who would show up in court to support me throughout the trial. I appreciated his kind words when things were not going so well.

With all appeals exhausted and the pending recall election on the horizon, Steve Pellino decided to call a special meeting of the Ridgefield Democratic County Committee. The issue on the table was who the committee would select to be placed on the ballot to serve as mayor if the recall question were answered in the affirmative. That is, if the majority of the voters decided that I should be recalled from office, who would be on the ballot to replace me. I wanted my name to be provided as the Democratic candidate. It might seem odd to be recalled and elected on the same ballot, but recall elections were confusing. In the early eighties, that exact thing happened. In West New York, the mayor had been on the ballot of a recall election. The voters answered yes to the question whether or not he should be recalled. For the second question, the voters reelected him to be the mayor. That was the first reason why I wanted my name to be on the ballot for the second question.

The second reason was public perception. If the Democratic County Committee selected me, it would show everyone that they had confidence that I could win this election, and that the only people who believed I should be recalled were the Republicans who pushed this whole effort and those who signed the petition.

However, most people I spoke with said they were misled by the person gathering signatures for the petition. In fact, one of my friends from high school whose name showed up on the petition was told the petition was to lower taxes. Another said that she had no idea what she had signed and when she learned what it was for, she immediately asked for her name to be removed. It wasn't.

At this point, my closest allies on the council and even the municipal chair had asked for my resignation. They said after seeing the recall petition and the names of the people who had signed, they assumed I could not win. I would not do that.

As the date of the county committee meeting approached, I began to speak to the members one by one. I thought if I could make my case in person, I would be able to get some support. I was wrong. It tuned out county committee member Matt Skelley, a supporter of the Zisa for School Board Committee, had been working the council. I believe he is the one who turned the opinion of the council against me. He was also at the county committee meeting explaining why I should not be on the ballot in the recall election. Skelley got his way. The committee decided another name would be submitted instead of mine, and the only supporter who wanted to keep me on the ballot was Marlene Caride, a loyal friend who would eventually become Ridgefield's first assemblywoman. Marlene and her family were part of a core group of supporters who showed up to support me, Catherine, and my mother as we went through the fire of trial by jury.

The committee did not select a replacement name for me at that meeting, but in the next few days, they scoured high and low to find someone. Initially they wanted Joseph Valente, a County Committeeman from District 5 and chair of the planning board, but he would withdraw. Javier Acosta eventually became his replacement. In the weeks following the county committee meeting, another meeting was called to talk about the upcoming campaign and strategy. The Democratic councilmembers met at Steve's office to decide how the campaign would be coordinated. We had to defeat the first question, but if it were not defeated, we had to make sure Javier won on the second. The second question was a choice between Javier, Vincentz, and Albert Gil, the independent candidate who had at one time been my supporter in trying to defeat the recall effort. He had been photographed by the press standing in front of my house with a bullhorn shouting to those who were protesting for me to resign from office.

Skelley argued that the entire Democratic organization should be distancing themselves from me and focusing on electing Javier. At one point he said that we should have won the election in 2009 but because of me, Phil and Hugo lost to two inferior candidates. I could not take it anymore and blurted out the truth. If Skelley had supported Phil, like he should have as a county committeeman, we would have garnered the thirty or so votes needed to get at least Hugo elected. Skelley began cursing and called Phil a moron and said we stabbed him in the back by not picking him to run for office. A near brawl ensued. Skelley stormed out of the meeting, and Steve had to restrain Russ.

The strategy session may have been a mess, but things somewhat worked out for me because at least they weren't abandoning me altogether. We all decided that the Democratic organization would campaign to vote no to the recall question and to vote for Acosta, should we lose on the first question. This would be very confusing to the voters, but it was the only strategy that could unify the two ideas.

The next day, I contacted my friend and former campaign adviser Jim Madden to discuss the strategy for the election. I did not have much money in my campaign fund, since I had not held a fundraiser in years. In fact, most of the fundraising I did over the past few years was for the local Democratic organization's candidates. Our plan was to put out a letter that focused on the fact that I was innocent and that I was entitled to a fair trial. I emphasized that Americans are innocent until proven guilty and thanked the voters for their support over the years and for their kindness during this most trying of times. I also let residents know about how the Republicans had not done anything to improve the town since the day of my arrest and instead had just focused on getting me out of office.

The other thing that I did was target my core voting block through constant text messaging. I had a website set up, along with a Facebook page, that would provide residents with the major issues of the campaign. I would post campaign updates on Facebook as I went door to door to discuss the election with local residents.

By joining forces with the Democratic organization, financing the election would be easier since they already had a war chest. The only thing I needed to raise money for was printing and mailing the letter. The Democratic organization would provide funding for the signs and the door to door handouts, along with any other expenses that were needed.

The signs were unusual since they said Vote No to Recall and Acosta for Mayor. I began to get questions about them almost immediately. People who did not like Javier wanted to know if they had to vote for him even though they would vote no to having me recalled. This cost me votes, since Javier had his group of enemies in town, as we all did. The big question was when you added his enemies to mine, would that be enough to defeat me and put Vincentz into office? That question would be answered on the day of the special election, which was scheduled for August 17, 2009.

The press had a field day. The local paper, the *Record*, continued to run article after article about me and the corruption case, along with other improprieties that the Republicans alleged had occurred while I was in office. No matter how baseless an allegation was, the press would run a story. On the day of the recall election, the *Record* ran an editorial called "Total Recall" about why I should be taken out of office.

I ran an unorthodox campaign and worked hard at it. I continued to keep my core supporters updated as to my status and to remind them to get out on election day. I went to the homes of my core voting group, the garden apartments, and the people Catherine and I knew well from our involvement in the school and recreation programs. I went door to door and campaigned with Hugo right through the weekend.

On the day of the election, I was primed to hit the town and pull out my votes. I awoke to a town in a media frenzy. When I put on the television, all the major networks were in Ridgefield reporting on the recall election. It was a slow time for the news since it was the dead of summer, and we were the only election taking place in the whole country. When I arrived at the Bergen Boulevard School to vote, I was stopped by a Fox News reporter. After voting, I immediately left the school because I had a lot of work to do. I went to the library, which was home to two of the town's voting districts and where I usually spent election days, shaking hands as people went to vote and waiting for the results. As I approached the library parking lot, 1010 WINS News pulled up, and a Channel 12 News van drove into the lot. I gave interviews to both of the stations and then took my post outside the library where I stayed most of the day, greeting people as they went into the library to vote. Most of them voiced their support for me and my campaign. The news people told me how surprised they were that I was getting so much support on this day. The media and the pundits had predicted a landslide victory for Vincentz.

All day, the New Jersey politics website politickernj.com had a reporter providing hour-by-hour commentary. Every move I made was documented, and all important and unimportant events during the course of the election were reported online. As the polls closed, we retired to Steve Pellino's law office, as we did every election day, to tally the results. The final numbers showed that I had beaten back the recall effort by about thirty votes. Hugo picked me up and carried me outside as the reporter from politickernj.com waited with a camera and photographed me being carried out in Hugo's arms. The reporter published the famous picture on the website the next day and quoted Jerry Ranieri, who was one of the election workers and a county committee member, saying that he wished he could see the look on Warren Vincentz's face now.

Unfortunately for the Republicans, they had set up the Ridgefield Community Center for a big celebration. The place was packed, and a reporter from politickernj.com was there too, reporting on what was supposed to be a victory party. Instead, it was a nightmare for Vincentz and company.

The quotes on the website for politickernj.com were classic: "Dear Jesus, he won?" "How could this have happened?" It was comical to see the people who hated me with a passion—for no other reason than the fact that I was a Democrat and had opposed their party's views for so long—taking ill as a result of my winning. How could I win an election with an indictment hanging over my head, when my party was split over its support for me, and in a year when the theme across the country was to throw all incumbents out of office because America was going down the wrong path?

Out of all the quotes from that evening, the one that would continue to haunt the Ridgefield Republican Organization for years to come came from the one and only Bob Avery, the former municipal court judge and councilmember. Bob's arrogance was demonstrated to everyone in Ridgefield and Bergen County when the *Record* picked up his quote from politickernj.com. Avery said that "Ridgefield voters have failed their collective intelligence test" by electing to keep me in office. That quote would serve as campaign fodder in the upcoming fall election and helped cost the Republicans election victories in the years to come, allowing me to be reelected by a wide margin of victory in 2011. In the end, it would cause a rift in the Republican organization.

We left Steve's office to celebrate our victory that evening, and instead of going to our usual location out of town, I told everyone I wanted to have a drink at Café Tivoli in Ridgefield, where we had not celebrated in some time. It was the perfect place right on Shaler Boulevard in Ridgefield. It was where the Republicans would normally gather but where Democrats originally had spent election nights, either in victory or in defeat.

The group assembled in the bar area on the first floor and as the drinks began to flow, I noticed a *Record* reporter enter along with someone I did not recognize. He was an *Associated Press* reporter, and they wanted an interview with me. I acquiesced. I told them that Ridgefield residents let the world know that I did not do anything wrong and that I was innocent. By keeping me in office under the most trying of circumstances, the residents showed their belief in me. I appreciated it and was moved by this gesture. I also said that this election was a vendetta by Bob Avery and the Republican organization, who would not stop until I was out of office. I did not realize that Avery and his goons would take things one step further by supplying information to the FBI and United States Attorney's Office of alleged illegal activity that I was engaged in, which was, of course, false and untrue.

As I finished the interview, the photographers took pictures of me with my family and then I sat down to have a slice of pizza and a beer. When I looked at the table, I noticed someone had ripped out the editorial from the *Record* that day, which essentially told residents to vote me out of office, and had written the words "HA HA" across the story. A photograph of that made its way onto politickernj.com, and I enjoyed looking at it every time I went online to read the story about how I beat the odds and won the election.

A friend of mine called me the next day to let me know that his brother lived in Idaho and that my election was being reported in Boise. The first time I entered into local politics, I never would have imagined that one of my campaigns would be a national news event. I was being discussed on radio talk shows. They debated whether or not someone should resign from office if they are presumed innocent and have not been convicted.

Should a prosecutor be able to tell politicians to get out of office and effectively undermine our representative process before a guilty verdict? I saw the relevance not only in my own life, but in the lives of those accused and falsely accused. Everyone should have their day in court before being convicted in the public, which made me even more determined to win the trial and get on with my life as a public servant.

The recall victory was a turning point and things were finally going in the right direction for me and my family. I was finally able to get a good night's sleep that evening. The next day, the newspaper reported the election as, "Suarez narrowly survives recall election." They didn't bother to tell how I had the public's support and beat the odds by becoming the first candidate to survive a recall election in New Jersey's history. But that is just how I expected the newspapers to tell it; don't let the facts get in the way of a good story.

Chapter 23

PREPARING FOR TRIAL

With the recall election behind me, I could now focus on the trial, which was less than two months away. The one benefit of the whole recall mess was that it became a distraction for me and my family as the trial date loomed in the distance, and now it was crunch time. Things were going to get interesting.

Judge Linares had scheduled motions for my trial and Vinny's to be heard at the same time. Mike and John took issue with this, along with Dwek's verbiage in his testimony in a previous trial. When Dwek had testified in the Beldini trial and described his meeting with Beldini, he called her a "corrupt public official," and used words like *bribe* when he referred to money he discussed at the meetings he was recording. Mike and John's issue was that these not only were inflammatory words which were unduly prejudicial and should not be mentioned at the time of Dwek's testimony, but that they were legal terms. A jury should be the ones to determine whether someone was a corrupt public official and whether there was a bribe. Judge Linares agreed and would carefully monitor Dwek's testimony during the course of my trial. This was such an effective strategy that it would be followed in all subsequent trials where Dwek would testify. In the Beldini case, it would be the basis for a motion for a new trial. Unfortunately for Beldini, the judge did not overturn the verdict.

Regarding the combined trials, Mike and John made a motion to have two separate trials. Vinny was being charged with money laundering along with the corruption charges in my case. Vinny had been washing money with Dwek long before I met him, and, naturally, without my knowledge, which is what the prosecution also admitted. Our argument was that the money laundering case would prejudice my case. Everyone would see Vinny as a real "bad guy" and wonder how I could have associated myself with him, possibly thinking I was guilty by association. Judge Linares agreed and severed the case in two. Vinny would later be subject to a separate trial on the money laundering allegations. The judge refused to sever Vinny completely from my case, though, and we would be tried as codefendants. Mike and John had wanted to avoid us being tried at the same time. The motion asked too much of the judge, and he denied that portion of the motion.

Next, Mike and John filed a motion that was more of a public relations move that had a slim chance of getting approval. They wanted the judge to admit as evidence a lie detector test that Vinny had taken and passed earlier in the year. From day one, Vinny insisted that he gave the alleged bribe money back to Dwek. Vinny said that on a specific day over the summer Dwek had gone to his office, and when he arrived they had a brief discussion wherein Vinny told Dwek that I did not want the money and that he went into a box behind his desk to get the cash and gave it to Dwek, who pocketed it. If Vinny was telling the truth, then Dwek committed yet another scam, this time against the very FBI he was supposedly helping, since he never returned the money to the FBI.

The lie detector test had to be rescheduled several times due to Vinny's health, but when he finally had it administered, he passed with flying colors. This proved that Vinny was not only telling the truth, but that he was honest. He testified that I refused to take the money and that he had given it back to Dwek. This proved that I did not take a bribe, yet the government still continued with the case. Now we were in open court that was being covered by the press. If this got out, it would make the government look bad. I think this is partly why the judge ruled that the lie detector test would not be admissible at the trial. We expected to lose that motion, but the headlines in the news the next day made the loss well worth the effort. Public opinion was based upon what people were reading, and as bad as the press had been for me, a story about a lie detector test that proved my innocence knocked the legs out of the prosecution's case, and the jury pool would be reading all about it.

Lastly, Mike and John asked for more tapes which had been provided but were damaged, along with new tapes that had not yet been provided. They also asked for text messages that Dwek and the FBI agents exchanged during the meetings at Patsy's. The government would search for this discovery and provide whatever they had.

The last item the judge covered was the trial date. It was going to be firm. Wisely, the judge and everyone agreed that the jury would be selected the week of October 5, 2010, and the following week the trial would start. Jury selection would be time-consuming and everyone agreed, taking several days to strategize before the trial. The next time I would see Judge Linares would be at jury selection.

We exited the courtroom, but only after I checked in with the pretrial officer, who was eagerly awaiting my arrival that month, one month closer to my being convicted and incarcerated and off her to-do list.

Mike, John, and I headed back to their office to discuss what had happened and the next steps. They wanted me to review the tapes and know them inside out. I had to know what was going on at the meetings and have an explanation for what was occurring without hesitation. We would also set up sample juries, made up of both people I knew and who did not know me. Mike and John would bring them to the office for a day so they could comment on what they saw and respond to what Mike and John were going to say. They would also have the opportunity to ask me questions, which would be invaluable for my case. It was a trial run. I would get to hear what people thought as they were watching the tapes and respond to the questions that they had, which also prepared me for what the federal prosecutor might ask at any given time.

The preparation process was exhaustive, but when you are talking about twenty years in jail, it is well worth every minute. None of us wanted to lose the case, and Mike would always assure me that so long as I followed what he told me to do, everything would be okay. In the end, he was right. But juries can be unpredictable and waiting for their decision can be maddening. I knew this from the civil trials that I had done. In one case, you expect to lose and you win; in another, you think that you have a great case only to be told by the jury that you were wrong.

After the court had ordered the government to provide us with all the evidence, the United States Attorney gave us numerous tapes that we had never known were in existence. They provided a massive number of recordings all mixed together. Mike and John had to cull through a lot of nonsense to find something involved in my case. The prosecutors underestimated Mike and John. John listened to every single audio tape, watched every video, and tried to decipher every inaudible and distorted tape. In fact, John found things the prosecutor never even knew were provided.

On one audio tape during another sting operation, FBI agents told Dwek to "dirty him up" as he went to a taped meeting. Obviously, the feds were encouraging Dwek to say incriminating things and engage in incriminating activity during a meeting to cement the case against some unsuspecting rabbi or politician.

After a complete review of the tapes, two things became apparent in my specific case: the feds were going all-in to get me, and even they did not think that their case was airtight. It was easy to reach this conclusion when listening to the audio tapes of Vinny and Dwek speaking to one another after my third and final meeting.

The first tape was of a phone conversation that took place when Dwek called Vinny to see if he could get another meeting with me after June 1, 2009. Vinny lied to Dwek, saying that he was going to get in touch with me but I was on vacation. Once I got back, Vinny said he would set up a meeting. Checking my schedule during the week that the phone conversation took place, I was not on vacation. Vinny had been calling me to set up another meeting with Dwek, but I refused to meet.

The next tape was of a meeting a few weeks later in June when Dwek called Vinny to see if we could get together and asked what the problem was. Vinny said that he just called my office and my secretary said I was out to lunch, but that another meeting would be scheduled. Again, I checked my schedule on the date that Vinny said I was out to lunch, and I was on vacation. Vinny never did call me. He correctly assumed that I did not want to talk to him or Dwek anymore, but apparently wanted to string Dwek along.

We saw video of a meeting at Vinny's office, where Dwek was still trying to get a meeting with me. Vinny said that he thought I was mad at him because I was not calling him back. Dwek was saying to give me more money, to give me a bank check, anything to lock me down. Vinny assured him that he would talk to me about it and that everything was okay.

Based upon the sheer number of calls between Dwek and Vinny, obviously at the direction of the FBI, the feds seemed hell-bent on entrapping me. Their aggressiveness would be used against both Dwek and Vinny at trial and would be one of the fatal blows to the case against me.

Finally, we learned the FBI made a run at Vinny in his apartment in the early morning hours of July 23, 2009. They were trying to get him to say something incriminating. Vinny didn't bite. This frustrated the feds even more. In fact, what we were able to obtain from the FBI's disclosure that they had to provide before the trial was that Vinny essentially made statements that exculpated my involvement in the crime. However, they did not provide this information until the very last moment.

Essentially, the feds had a very weak case against me. It seemed like they believed they could throw a public official in front of a jury and secure a conviction. John once told me that if this were not a public corruption case against an elected official, it would never have been brought. Once we were in the case though, it was up to the jury to set me free. That was just how they operated.

As I readied for the trial that was about to begin, there was a calm that came over me. I finally was going to be able to tell everyone what had happened, whether the jury believed me or not. The support that my family, friends, and residents of Ridgefield were giving me in the final push to the trial was incredible and gave me the energy that I needed to get through the next month. I looked at the trial as the last part of the nightmare and finally saw the end of the tunnel. The light was now shining to save me and my family.

Chapter 24

TRIAL BY FIRE

A few days prior to jury selection, the prosecution and defense exchanged witness lists and agreed on a summary of the case. The list that we provided was all encompassing. We didn't want to leave anyone out that may be called. The prosecution did the same. Looking over the prosecution's list, it seemed like a who's who of people who hated me in Ridgefield. Mike and John relished the idea of the prosecution parading my political enemies in court. They said it would make the whole case look like a political prosecution.

When we showed up for the first day of jury selection, Judge Linares suggested both sides use an agreed-upon questionnaire to pre-screen the jurors. This would be a list of questions that would be asked of the jurors to see whether they were biased one way or another, for or against the prosecution or the defense. This procedure would make things go quicker in terms of jury selection. Rather than having the judge doing all the questioning in open court with each individual juror, which could take weeks, it would allow all the jurors to be questioned at the same time. Judge Linares gave us the format of the questions he had used in the Beldini trial, and we tweaked them to our liking for my case.

There was nothing unusual about the questions. They were about the potential juror's job, address, educational background, view on law enforcement. They delved into whether they would believe the testimony of a law enforcement officer over that of a lay witness, inquired about their past experiences with law enforcement, their view of politicians in New Jersey, and whether or not they believed someone was innocent until proven guilty.

After both sides agreed upon the questions, the judge took the bench and called in the potential jurors. We stood while the jurors entered the courtroom. The lawyers involved in the case began sizing up the jury pool at once, to see who they wanted or did not want on the jury. The judge had us sit, and the process of choosing twelve people along with four alternates from the pool of hundreds of potential jurors commenced. I had always enjoyed jury selection when picking my civil juries of six members and two alternates, but this was not a pleasant experience.

As the day went on and one day turned into two days and two days turned into three, a jury was eventually seated that was satisfactory to both sides. Judge Linares then dismissed everyone for the week. The trial would start on the following Monday, giving Mike and John time to make final preparations to do battle. Somehow, I dreamt that the case would still be dismissed by the prosecution, but it was not. The media circus on jury selection day was not that bad, and I hardly remember any news media at the courthouse other than an occasional photographer and maybe a short story in the paper that jury selection had begun and that the trial was scheduled for Monday, October 12, 2010.

The Sunday before the trial was to begin, John told me to invite a couple of friends to his office so he could go over his opening statement. I asked my brother-in-law Rich Bani and Councilman Russ Castelli. The opening was all-encompassing and very thorough. Rich and Russ thought it was very good and had only a few comments. John made some minor revisions, and we were ready to go. I did not need any additional preparation, so we all left the office.

When I got home, I realized it was only one day until the final episode of this mess was to take place. Not knowing what to expect, I watched the Giants game that night and went to bed at around eleven thirty after watching my favorite television show, *Seinfeld*, which often relaxed me in the evening. I had been concerned about not getting a good night's sleep during the trial, since I had never been a good sleeper, but both Catherine and I slept better than ever during the course of the trial, mostly because of mental exhaustion from the day's events.

When I got up, I followed the schedule that would take place Monday through Friday until the end of the trial. I would hit my treadmill at about seven and then help get the kids ready for school. Then I would leave for Newark by eight o'clock. Leaving at that time, I would miss the morning traffic jam and usually park my car around nine, which was half an hour before court would start.

Catherine would drop off the kids at school, and Shelly would pick her up every day at about eight thirty. They would both arrive in the courtroom just prior to the trial starting and sit in the front row to watch the proceedings and give valuable input and moral support.

When I got to court, the circus was there: photographers, reporters, gawkers, and onlookers. There was even a reporter from the *Record* who was specially assigned to the case and blogged about it from the courtroom. The press would not leave a stone unturned throughout the process. The *Record* even had one of their editorial writers, Mike Kelly, show up one day. He must have stayed for all but twenty minutes and wrote a whole editorial during the trial about the impropriety of my meeting with Dwek at a restaurant in a seedy neighborhood. Although he got his facts wrong, that did not stop him from putting out a story that could bias the jury and damage my reputation.

As I entered the courtroom, I noticed many government employees and a large video screen set up at one end of the room. The prosecution was playing parts of the tapes. The FBI agent who escorted me on my perp walk when I was arrested was sitting with the prosecution. His face was well known in Ridgefield as the Republicans used it on all their campaign flyers in 2009 and in 2010. The prosecution also had a technical support person who was playing the tapes and rewinding them at the direction of McCarren and Nakly, the two assistants who were trying the case. There were many FBI agents, assistants, and supervisors from the government who would come and go during the course of the trial. My case was serious business for them, and they wanted to win at all costs. Since the government had not lost a political corruption case in ten years, and after two hundred convictions, I wasn't going to break their streak. Not to mention there were still many cases left from the sting that would be placed in jeopardy if I were to win.

As the time neared for the start of the trial, Catherine arrived with Shelley and I felt more at ease. My mother also showed up, as she did every day, along with her support group of various friends that would come to court with her daily. These people kept my mother calm and bore witness to the insanity that was going on in our lives. I was also fortunate to have a steady flow of friends that visited me at the courthouse throughout the course of the trial. My partner Ron Dario was there every day. Ron's wife, Lorraine, and both of their respective parents came throughout the proceedings. My sister-in-law was there with Catherine in the front row every day to offer her support. My sisters, nephew, brother-in-law, friends from decades ago, and newly found friends from the borough of Ridgefield also stopped by on occasion.

I was also happy to have the support of my police department; various officers would show up from time to time to show support. John told me that I had more people in court to support me than he had ever seen in any of the cases he had been trying throughout his entire career. It made me feel good to see so many people come to Newark and offer their kind words.

As for Vinny, he always had Annette and his lawyer in court. I would see him every morning in the hallway seated in his wheelchair. I would only nod at him, as I was told not to talk to Vinny because there were cameras everywhere and a simple "Good morning, how are you feeling?" could be construed by the prosecution as witness tampering, subjecting me to the threat of years in jail.

Prior to the start of the case, there was still an open issue of the text messages that Dwek had been sending to the FBI. Where were they and what did they say? The prosecution admitted that Dwek texted the FBI agents before, during, and after my meetings with him, hundreds of times over, but they claimed they did not preserve the messages. This was a major issue because it was obvious that when I would tell Dwek something he did not like, he would immediately get on his Blackberry and start texting. I knew in my heart that Dwek was telling the agents that I was not taking the bait and that he was concerned about the set up.

The judge ordered a special hearing on the text messages and the FBI's policy toward preservation of them, which took place at the end of the first week. The FBI was required to bring in all the agents involved in my investigation and the head of the FBI's technical department from Washington, DC. So as not to delay the trial, the case would proceed before the hearing.

The trial then commenced, and McCarren opened for the prosecution. He essentially laid out what we all knew was their case. He said that I was a corrupt public official, Vinny was my bagman, and that I took money from Dwek through Vinny in exchange for official action. McCarren said that this was all on tape and that is how they would prove their case. He spoke about the government's prime witness, Dwek, and how Dwek was not a "good guy" but that the government had to use people like this in order to get criminals. This was a common strategy among trial lawyers. They would expose their own witness' weaknesses to the jury before their adversary did in order to blunt the shock value of the cross-examination. The only problem for the government was that even they did not know what had been uncovered by my lawyers, and McCarren was about get an education on cross-examination that only Mike Critchley could give.

When McCarren was done with his opening, it was our turn. John laid out our case in a very simple and understandable way. I never took Dwek's money; I never made any promises to Dwek;

and there was no violation of law. The prosecution did not have all the facts, and this was their first glimpse into our defense.

With the opening arguments over, the government called their first witness: Solomon Dwek. As Dwek entered the courtroom, my wife explained to me afterward how a certain aura of evil could be felt. He had shaved his beard and was still wearing his yarmulke, which I am sure upset members of the Jewish community. Here was a man who thieved like Satan while still trying to look like he was following the tenets of an organized religion. I was embarrassed for him.

As Dwek took the witness stand, it was obvious that he was quirky. He kept touching his yarmulke like it was a nervous tick while answering questions from the prosecution. Judge Linares made sure that Dwek would not overstep his bounds by answering questions using terms like "corrupt" or "bribe" as he did in the Beldini and Van Pelt cases. Dwek ran over the defense attorneys in those prior cases by blurting out terms which were legal conclusions that a jury would have to decide, not him. It was obvious that the feds coached him well before taking the witness stand, and that he was well experienced in testifying on the stand. He narrated the tapes, describing his interpretation as to what had happened during the course of our three meetings.

By the end of the day the prosecution was finished with Dwek, confident that they had essentially made their case. Judge Linares asked if the defense wanted to start cross-examination or wait until tomorrow. Mike rose from his seat and said that he wanted to start right then and there, even though we all expected Dwek's testimony to continue into the next day. This was a strategic move on Mike's part because in criminal trials once the witness is finished testifying under direct examination, he then gets "turned over" to the defense and the prosecution can no longer speak with that witness until cross-examination is over. So, the FBI and McCarren would not have another night to prepare Dwek for Mike's cross.

Mike rose from his seat and approached Dwek. John had once told me that whatever happened to me as a result of the trial—win, lose, or draw—Mike's cross would cause Judge Linares to tack on at least five years to Dwek's sentence. I thought I was about to learn what that meant as the great Mike Critchley began to put on a clinic for the rest of the bar of New Jersey on how to conduct the cross-examination of a sociopath. But that would not happen this day, as Mike was not quite ready to school the court. He began with some simple questions for Dwek before asking the judge if we could break to continue the next day.

When we arrived in court the next day, the courtroom was packed with a who's who of the white-collar defense bar, along with most of the United States Attorney's Office. They all wanted to witness the master at work, and he did not disappoint. Mike started by going after Dwek on the past crimes he had committed, even those that the United States Attorney's Office did not know about. He got Dwek to admit that he had committed thousands of crimes.

Mike next moved onto the lies that Dwek had told while he was testifying for the prosecution during my trial. Dwek testified that he stopped lying and committing crimes when he became a confidential informant for the feds, but that was not true. He had failed to file income tax returns while working for the feds and lied on the stand during my trial when he said he had permission to not file the returns.

Mike was able to get Dwek to make certain admissions that implicated his wife, Pearl Dwek, for the crimes he was committing. Mike was moving so fast and hitting Dwek so hard that McCarren and Nakly did not know what to do, since they could not object to the questions and were left to watch their witness' credibility and likeability go south fast. It was so bad that the jurors would not even look at Dwek, and whenever they entered from a courtroom break, they made sure that they were far away from him because he was so despicable.

After more than two days of cross examination, Mike left Dwek a bloody mess, nothing but a blob on the witness stand that could not be revived through the prosecution's redirect. With his job done, Dwek slithered off the witness stand and out the courtroom doors, eager to testify in the next trial where he could try to take years off of his sentence by helping the feds convict another Bid Rig III defendant. It was too late, though. The damage was done. In fact, the feds would now second-guess ever using Dwek as their witness since he was now exposed as a Ponzi schemer on par with Bernie Madoff.

The next two witnesses that the prosecution put on the stand did not help their case at all. The first was the director of New Jersey Election Law Enforcement Commission (ELEC), whose testimony was suspect for both Judge Linares and my defense team. Why would the prosecutor bring in a witness to testify about a campaign fund when the donation in question was for a legal defense fund not regulated by ELEC? The prosecution said they would not delve into the area of my campaign account and Dwek's donation since it was irrelevant to the issue at hand. Once the prosecution called the ELEC witness, Nakly started to question on the area that Judge Linares just told her not to explore, and she ended the line of questioning.

The last prosecution witness was my legal defense fund accountant, Gary Stetz, who did not help the prosecution, and at the conclusion of his testimony the prosecution rested its case.

We finally got our turn to put on a defense. Before we did, the hearing regarding the text messages had to take place, and the court recessed for the day, allowing the proceeding involving this issue to be conducted first thing in the morning.

When we arrived at court in the morning, the prosecution had flown the head of the technology unit of the FBI to Newark to testify, and he was questioned by yet another Assistant United States Attorney. The testimony of the agent was preposterous, as he claimed that the FBI did not have the ability to store the text messages on their servers even though this was an ongoing investigation. The FBI was supposed to preserve this type of material under any other circumstances.

The next three witnesses were the special FBI agents who were Dwek's handlers while he was serving as a confidential witness during the sting. Judge Linares asked that the witnesses be sequestered so as not to taint the testimony of one another during the direct and cross-examination. As the first witness testified, via telephone since he was in Afghanistan, something happened that cemented my belief that Critchley was the King Kong of all attorneys. Mike noticed that McCarren had left the courtroom to go into the hallway while John was cross-examining the witness. With that, Mike went into the hallway and moments later charged into the courtroom, notifying the judge that McCarren was conferring with the agent who was sequestered in the hallway and admitted that he was telling the agent what was being said in court.

As McCarren charged into the courtroom, a furious Judge Linares asked McCarren if this was true. McCarren apologized and admitted to the witness tampering. Judge Linares, visibly upset, said that he would address this issue at another time, as the second and third witnesses took the stand and were questioned about the missing text messages.

When everything was over, Judge Linares' decision was favorable to the defense but did not give us everything we wanted. Mike had initially moved that Dwek's testimony be stricken from the record, but the judge thought that this was an extreme remedy, and, instead, he opted for an adverse inference charge to be read to the jury at the end of the case. Mike could now argue to the jury that since the FBI had destroyed the texts when they had a duty not to, the jury could infer that the information in them was favorable to me.

I was the next witness to testify, and John would be doing my direct. I told the truth to the jury, and when McCarren took over to cross-examine me, I just answered his questions truthfully.

As I continued testifying the next day, I just kept telling the truth on the stand, which made it difficult for McCarren to cross-examine since my actions were never a crime. You can never make someone look bad when they tell the truth, since the story never changes. I had an explanation for everything, and the prosecution's portrayal of events was not as ominous as had been inferred from the beginning of the case. When I was done testifying, my good friend and civil trial attorney Eric Harrison told Mike that this was the best I had been on the stand. Eric knew what he was talking about, since he had seen me testify twice before, once in defense of the borough in federal court and once in state court.

The next witness was Catherine, and she was so good on direct examination that there was no cross by the prosecution. We decided not to call any character witnesses, since she was as good a character witness as I could have while also testifying as to the facts of the case and what she knew.

Our last witness was regarded by some friends in the audience as the best one we had offered. Henry Klingeman took the stand and testified that he had advised me on the legal defense fund. He said that I had immediately came to see him after I met with Dwek, asking for his advice and that I followed it to a *T*. He also showed the check for ten thousand dollars that Vinny had given to me. He confirmed that I had given him the check, and he then advised me to meet with Vinny and Dwek only to make it clear that I follow the law with everything I did. Henry also affirmed that he advised me that so long as I knew that Vinny wanted to give to the legal defense fund, I could accept money from him.

McCarren's cross of Henry was ineffective and, in many ways, helped me to attain the acquittal that we were looking for. McCarren started by asking Henry why he would not speak with the United States Attorney's Office about me when he knew these facts. Henry's response was that under the rules of professional conduct he had an ethical obligation to me as his client not to speak with prosecutors who were trying to put me in jail. He also said that I had not waived the attorney-client privilege prior to the trial.

That sent McCarren into a tizzy, and he asked Henry if he just tried to put people in jail or seek justice when he was an assistant United States Attorney. Henry told McCarren that he hoped *he* was trying to seek justice. The jury looked like they were shocked that the prosecutor was trying to put me in jail for this case.

My defense rested at that point, and then Vinny's trial began. Vinny's attorney, Anthony Kress, had been doing a good job throughout the trial and essentially supported the defense that I had been providing. To his credit, Vinny took the stand and told the jury that I knew nothing about the scheme he and Dwek had cooked up, and that I never accepted money from Dwek. When Vinny said that I would never take a bribe, as I was an ethical person, the prosecution objected. He went on to say that I was a straight arrow. Vinny also testified that he gave the money back to Dwek and gave specific information as to when and where the exchange took place. This put the prosecution on its heels.

When McCarren cross-examined Vinny, he pulled out everything he had to make Vinny look like a liar. Vinny admitted that he had been lying to Dwek in order to stay in his good graces so that he would have exclusive rights to all of Dwek's real estate listings.

The case was over, and the only things left were the closing arguments by the prosecution and the defense. The prosecutor went first and hit the issues Nakly raised during the trial to establish the elements of the crime.

At the beginning of my case it was agreed that John would do the opening and Mike would do the closing. Eddy Denoia from Mike's office, who was a very good attorney, was in court that day to help set up the PowerPoint presentation, and John was going to help Mike organize the information that needed to be presented. Just as we were going to start, John was notified that one of his clients had just been arrested and was appearing in another courtroom for his first appearance. The timing of this was suspect, as John said the other case had been going on for a while, and he never thought that the news would come on this day. As a result, John had to leave the courtroom and Eddy and Mike would have to get through the closing without John's assistance.

As one attorney who watched from the audience said, Mike's closing was one for the ages. One of the jurors began crying as Mike told of how one day I was on top of the world, and the next I was in the middle of a nightmare because of the way I trusted people. Mike told the jury that I did not suspect that someone like Dwek would be out in the world trying to take advantage of me and my office.

Mike's closing went on for one half a day, and he used the PowerPoint presentation very effectively. A who's who of attorneys was in the audience watching the master in his element, and at the end of the closing, after he shredded Dwek's credibility, he whispered to the jury, "Anthony came here an innocent man. I have taken him as far as I can go. I am now turning him over to you. Take care of him." Silence fell in the courtroom. The prosecution had a chance to offer a rebuttal and then Judge Linares dismissed the jury to their room to begin their deliberations.

The jury began to deliberate on Friday afternoon. At one point, we all thought that there would be a verdict by the end of the day. However, it would not be that easy for me, and the jury asked to come back the next week.

When we returned to court on Monday, the jury had questions and then more questions. They went on and on. The days went on and on. During deliberations, another political corruption trial that had been going on in the courtroom next to Judge Linares involving the former mayor of Perth Amboy had ended with a guilty verdict.

On Wednesday, as the jury entered its fourth day of deliberations, my entire entourage had enough of the waiting.

We wondered what could be taking so long. We had all assumed that the jury had me down as innocent the previous Friday, and that they were deliberating over whether or not to convict Vinny.

Finally, at about two in the afternoon on Wednesday there was a verdict. Everyone scurried to the courtroom from the hallway. Judge Linares was away at a conference, so another judge sat in his place. When we all assembled at the defense table and the prosecutors were seated in their respective spots, the judge called in the jury.

The jury forewoman was asked to rise and render the verdict. As I stood, I could feel the air coming out of my mouth as the forewoman read "Not guilty" to all of the charges against me. I began to cry and hugged Mike and John. Everyone behind me erupted in cheers. The news wasn't as good for Vinny, who was found guilty of offering a corrupt payment and attempted bribery. Annette began to cry, and Catherine hugged her.

We exited the courtroom and went right to the lawyer's lounge to gather our thoughts. My cell phone went crazy with text message after text message congratulating me. The small group who was there when the verdict came in was made up of the core members of the support team who always came to court to wish me and my family well. It consisted of my mom, Eric Harrison, David Ciccolella, and Ron Dario. Shelly was not there, as she had to go to state court that afternoon, so she missed the whole thing, but she caught up with me in the parking lot afterward to hug me and Catherine and wish us well.

When we left the lawyer's lounge and exited the building, the press was there to question me. I thanked Mike and John, the residents of Ridgefield, and my family and friends for supporting me throughout the ordeal. The happiness on my face was apparent on the covers of the *Record* and *Star Ledger* newspapers, both of which ran front page stories of my victory the next day. One question from the *Record* reporter was whether I would ever go to Patsy's again. "Of course," I said. "They have great fish." Some of the people nearby laughed.

As we left to go our separate ways, a photographer took a poignant photo of Catherine and me under an umbrella as it started to rain. You could see a man next to me as we walked down the street to get into our car. It was the back of my partner, Ron Dario, who through the whole trial came to see me every day, and right up until the end believed in my innocence.

When we left Newark, Catherine and I stopped by my law office for a celebratory drink. We were greeted by Councilmen Castelli and Acosta, who had arranged for a victory party at Don Quijote, a Spanish restaurant right next door to Patsy's. We left my office and went to pick up our children, who were staying with our friend, Theresa Patti. As soon as Theresa opened the door, she hugged Catherine and me. Once we saw Matthew and Laura inside the house, our emotions got the best of us. We hugged both of them and began to cry.

That night, Don Quijote was packed with supporters and family who wanted to see me and tell me that they always believed in my innocence and wanted to wish me well. Ridgefield police officer Lieutenant William Pych brought a sign that he had in his front lawn throughout my ordeal. The sign stated in bold letters "Innocent Until Proven Guilty." He put the sign facedown on a table and people who attended the party signed it with their well wishes. That sign hung in my law office as a constant reminder of the good in the people of Ridgefield.

Chapter 25

VINDICATION BY ELECTION

When I awoke the day after the verdict, it felt like a five-hundred-pound weight was lifted off of my chest. I could breathe again. With all our focus for the past couple of months being on the trial, the general election had crept up on us. During the summer, I did go door to door with our local candidates Hugo Jimenez, who was making his second run for borough council, and Ray Penabad. Ray was a decent man who supported the party line that I should resign before the recall election. On the night that I won the recall, he apologized and said how badly he felt. I appreciated his sincerity.

My offer to go door to door was accepted insofar as we only went to my staunch supporters, where I would mostly be asked questions about how my family and I were doing. After a few weeks of campaigning, I focused on writing the campaign flyers. It was a great way to take my mind off the trial, from which I was still having flashbacks. I wrote some of my best literature during this time because Nicholas Lonzisero was up for reelection, and I had a lot to say about him and his abilities.

The Republicans continued their scare tactics and sent out literature with me and my attorneys on the cover, claiming that if just one Democrat won the election, the town would foot my multi-million-dollar legal bill. They never said what they wanted to do to make Ridgefield a better place to live; instead, they continued to attack me personally.

Their tactic did not work. Lonzisero lost his bid for reelection to Hugo, although his running mate, Severino, beat Ray by a narrow margin of victory. As a result, the council would be split in the coming year, and I would be the tie breaker. Ironically, I went from being a mayor with no power to one that wielded all the power in one election cycle. The *Record* reported it the next day as, "Suarez Gets Payback" not "Voters Vindicate Suarez Again," but what else could I have expected?

On election night we celebrated Hugo's victory, and people came out again to Don Quijote, congratulating the local party leadership as we braced for a year of being in the majority and doing what was best for the town.

Hugo's victory reaffirmed that the residents of Ridgefield believed my ideas were the right ones for the town. It was less than two weeks since the verdict, which made the election even more satisfying. The Republicans had realized their worst nightmare:

I was vindicated, and the Democrats took the majority on the council less than two weeks later. Suddenly, people who had not called me in over a year wanted to speak with me again, and I became the focus of the county Democratic leadership in the year to come.

Things were once again good in Ridgefield, and the residents demonstrated their support for my team by showing up at the January 2011 reorganization meeting in droves to cheer us on. We tackled the issues that mattered most to Ridgefield for the next year. Ironically, 2011 was the last year of my term as mayor and Javier and Russ were also up for election.

I did not intend to run for reelection after I won my second term. Since the Republicans had made most of my second term a nullity, after talking it over with Catherine, and getting her approval, I decided to give it another shot and declared my candidacy after months of soul searching.

My decision was bolstered by two things: First, the Democrats were in the majority. This would allow me to move my agenda forward. Second, the group of Democratic councilmen that I was working with cooperated with one another more than any other group that I had served with in over ten years. The potential was encouraging, so I decided in March that I would make another run for reelection.

During the course of the year, the Democratic councilmen and I focused on saving money and scaling back the budget that had been inflated by our opponents giving out jobs to campaign workers and friends. The residents responded in force as we won reelection by three hundred votes, my biggest victory margin since 2003. It was nearly triple my last reelection victory, and ten times the difference in the recall election.

We were bolstered in our election victory by the fact that the Republican party was now split. Half the party wanted Avery out and the other half wanted him to remain as the municipal chairman. There was a heated Republican primary election, which caused the rift and fighting to continue well into the fall.

The November 2011 election victory was big for Ridgefield on another front. Marlene Caride, the woman who had supported me to the end, the only county committee member that thought my name should be on the ballot for the recall election, and the friend who appeared in court with her family to show support during my corruption trial, had just won election as assemblywoman from Ridgefield. The borough would have its first assemblywoman in history, and she would be the first Latina to hold the seat in District 36. She came to the reorganization meeting in January to swear me in and to say some kind words. We gave her a rousing round of applause for her accomplishment when she was announced.

Many people from my past showed up at our reorganization meeting in January 2012 to join in savoring my victory over Warren Vincentz. I drove to the Community Center that night with my wife and children, ready to be sworn in to my third term. As I entered the packed building, well-wishers were everywhere.

While I worked my way to the dais to start the meeting and sit down, I looked into the crowed of faces. Some were so happy that they were crying, others were so angry I had won the election that they could barely contain their frustration.

John Vazquez was in the audience with his two daughters. As I looked at him and his children, I could not help but think about what could have happened to my family and me if the jury had not gotten it right. My mind flashed quickly back to the day that the FBI agent called me in Long Beach Island to say there was a warrant for my arrest; being held in that jail cell with a bunch of politicians and rabbis; protesters and news media swarming all over my house for publicity and a story; going to court for months on end during the time the charges were still pending against me; and the night of the recall election, when I made history thanks to the people of Ridgefield by being the first Mayor to ever win such a contest.

I thought about all the time that I had to spend fighting the false charges, and how it took up most of my and my family's life for eighteen months. As I thought about it and wondered whether getting into politics was worth all of that, I looked into the audience and I saw my mom, stepfather, wife, children, and friends, who had all come to support me. I smiled and picked up the gavel that I had been using over the past eight years to start the meetings of the Mayor and Council, banged it onto the table, and called the meeting to order.

EPILOGUE

I often look back on the date of the arrest, which is captured for posterity on the internet so that even though our children may not remember what happened, they will be able to see and read about what happened to their father. I have been a changed person since the whole experience, becoming more like Mike and John, looking to cover myself in all situations and never attending meetings unless there are many witnesses present, which I would never have done in the past.

I have to say that this change is not for the better; I have become more suspicious and untrusting, less tolerant with those who do not understand. One thing that has not changed though is my commitment to making things better for the residents of Ridgefield.

As I write this book, the Bid Rig III case is history. Leona Beldini was denied her last shot at trying to have a new trial but has since been released; Dennis Elwell, the mayor of Secaucus who was convicted after my case, was sentenced to two and a half years in jail; and Lou Manzo, a defendant in the case, had Judge Linares throw the case out of court and sued the feds to get his attorney's fees reimbursed. He lost that one. Manzo claims that his life has been put in shambles as a result of the arrest and blames Christie for everything. He wrote a book on the sting.

The Jersey Sting is another book about the operation, but the writers did not have first-hand knowledge of what really happened, and I consider their work one of fiction, as the people who fed the authors the information were from the United States Attorney's Office. That office wouldn't give all the information that I became privy to as I went through the process.

The one thing you learn to appreciate as you go through the worst of times is who your real friends are, and they were there for me every step of the way. In a sense, I never felt lonely even though this was the loneliest period of my life.

When I moved to my new law office in Hackensack in November 2011, I met our new Federal Express delivery man. He was one of the jurors in my case, and when he saw the firm's name he asked for me. He wanted to see how I was doing and told me he was one of the jurors who had held out for me and my innocence. I told him I was grateful for his belief in me and appreciated his concern for my family.

I sometimes think of how close I came to losing my life as I knew it because of the bogus charges that were leveled against me. I wonder if giving my time and effort to help make the borough of Ridgefield a great place to live and risk being pursued by the federal government for crimes that I did not commit just because I was an attractive target was worth it. Mayors going to jail are a lot better for the newspapers than your low-level drug dealers.

Dwek was sentenced to six years. A light sentence by any means considering everything he did. The feds wanted him to receive an even lighter sentence, but Judge Linares did not go for their recommendation. He knew what type of person Dwek was from my trial. And Chris Christie won reelection as governor of New Jersey. Looking back, I wonder if Christie realizes the he would have beaten Corzine in the 2009 Gubernatorial election even without the Bid Rig III sting.

As for my attorneys, John Vazquez was nominated by President Obama to be a federal judge in New Jersey. I was able to attend his swearing in ceremony, along with a number of federal prosecutors. Chris Christie was there, and I avoided him while going to shake Judge Vazquez's hand in his courtroom.

Mike Critchley went on to represent another high-profile client, Bridget Ann Kelly, who was charged with violating federal criminal laws in the George Washington Bridge scandal, which came to be known as Bridgegate. Kelly was convicted but Bridgegate, in the eyes of many, exposed Christie as a bully, costing him a run for the presidency and causing him to become the least popular governor in New Jersey history.

As for the two Assistant US Attorneys who prosecuted me, I know they were just doing their jobs. They both seemed to be decent, intelligent people who had no personal animus towards me. They wanted to win their case. Unfortunately, both were involved in the matter because the office had been run by a man who tainted everything he could for his personal benefit. What I find incredible is the influence Christie had over others during his tenure as US Attorney for the District of New Jersey. Christie not only fooled the people of New Jersey into thinking that he was looking out for them, but he was also able to manipulate the press to his advantage.

In the end, justice prevailed, but it has had a profound effect on me and my family. We will never be the same, but one thing will never change and that is my belief in the people of the state of New Jersey. They were the ones who acquitted me, believed me, and gave me my life back.

ACKNOWLEDGMENTS

This book was written over a period of several years, and continuously updated and edited up until the time of its publication. I began writing it after the verdict in 2010, when I got up before everyone else in the morning.

Writing the book was a form of therapy for me, allowing me to highlight the injustices that I believe I came across during the time period that it covers, many of which I still see playing out against others to this day. With the help of the people below I was able to complete the book.

All my love and thanks to Catherine for allowing me the time to sit down and write, rewrite, edit, and reedit this book, telling a story that needed to be told.

Thanks to my mom for her constant support and reminders of events that I wrote about in the book.

Thanks to Charles Salzberg from the New York Writer's Conference for all of his help and support.

Thanks to my editor Geoff Stone for his invaluable input and help in making the book what it is today.

Thanks to John Consoli for all of his help.

Thanks to my sister-in-law Nora Bani for the time she put in to review the book before it went to publication.

Many thanks to my friend Steve Pellino for his review of the book and suggestions.

And finally, thanks to the people at Mascot Books for their help and assistance in bringing the book to publication.